Becoming Conscious in a Corporate World

Without Losing Your Sanity

Lindsay Mastro

Woods Edge Press

INTRO

Holy shit. You found it. Hidden in the vast aisles of endless reads about leadership development, business growth, women in leadership, and spirituality - you found the book that gets you. You've worked your way through the corporate labyrinth with strengths in knowledge, influence, empathy, and strength. Maybe you recently got a promotion, maybe you've been in a leadership role for some time and are looking for the next thing to push you forward. Ultimately, you're looking for the thing that's going to bring fulfillment and offer a renewed sense of authenticity and purpose in your work and life.

You've always believed in something magical. You've had an enhanced level of intuition that's guided you through your life for as long as you can remember - or maybe you forgot. Maybe you've had a few unexplained experiences that always reassured you there was more to this life than just the day to day capitalist driven niceties, that you - admittedly - really enjoy. But at the same time you're planning your team strategy or tabbing through spreadsheets, you're thinking about your next escape to the garden or the woods.

This book is for you. The magically practical business leader, looking for a no bullshit way to incorporate your intuition and gifts into your leadership. To become a conscious leader who is well respected in your organization for your level headedness, your strength, your tenacity, but also your ability to make shit happen, while remaining connected to the universe within and surrounding you. Most importantly, while being unapologetically, authentically you.

So, how is this going to work? How are you going to bridge this vast gap of spirituality and the workplace? You'll do it by using the energies and strengths that are surrounding you. I hear you. You're like, "Ok, I want some hard tangible advice here - I don't need yet another book about auras and energy."

In the words of our fictional friend Maui, "What can I say, except... you're welcome."

As you work your way through this book, you'll come to understand how to use energetic and esoteric concepts like the lunar (moon) phases, the Hindu chakras, and spiritualism to specifically enhance your leadership and operations strategies to become a more Conscious

Leader.   There's really 3 things you'll need to do to make your way towards that goal; Heal, Align, and Cultivate.

Before you can apply these energy concepts in any real effective way in your work, you'll need to first focus on finding your own intuitive gifts, and get yourself back to homeostasis.   Once you quiet the noise and chaos of your world, you will have the space to truly become the authentic, whole, you. Heal first, baby.

Part 1: Heal

What you need to know about healing

First step to healing is to seek your own internal balance before addressing anyone on the outside.   Everyone wants to jump right into being their best selves, but the healing journey is a twisty turny windy road.   Some days you feel absolutely fantastic, like the 'stars have aligned' and nothing can bring you down.   Other days you might feel like you have absolutely no idea what you're doing, and honestly, might feel a little slighted that you've put in so much work, to feel so down.   It's easy to think that 'becoming healed' is as gorgeous as it looks on all those hippie boho instagram feeds, but it's all a balance.   Yin and Yang. Black and white.

The key to becoming healed is not to always be happy. It's a crazy mix of self-awareness, recognizing your past trauma and conditioning, learning to understand energy (internal and external), creating and maintaining boundaries, and learning about different tools and modalities that will help you on those days that you feel like you're stepping backwards. It's about living with intention; never taking a moment for granted, and seeing the big picture in life.

Lucky for you, this book includes tips on intuition, crystals, tools for your workspace, setting the vibe, setting intentions and goal setting all while rockin' your day job. All will help unlock the doors to your healing so you can begin to live a soul-aligned life.

Part 2: Align & Cultivate

Align your life with your own unique vibration

Once you've understood your pathways to healing, you decide what you'd like your life to be like. You'll do this a number of ways. First, you'll create your own mission for your life by thinking about what you'd like to achieve today, this month, and this year. Your goals and actions will change, but your value set will not.

Once you have a vision of what your ideal life looks like, you can determine what you allow in and what no longer fits. Is it your job that's holding you back from this? Is it your parents? Is it your spouse? Is it your boss? Is it your friends? On the flip side, who and what is currently in your life that supports your ideal day? Keep the good ones with you and get the not so good ones out.

I get it - some people you can't just 'get out'. BUT (a real big BUT here), you can establish boundaries, communicate your needs, avoid situations that you know might trigger you, and lean on those that support you to get through those difficult days and situations. We can't change others' behaviors, but we can protect our peace and show the impact it makes on our lives. Showing this strength changes the perspectives of others (and encourages the ones that are not aligned to get TF out.)

I'll show you how your moods, strengths, and daily activities can be tracked along the lunar cycle. Once you've tracked your patterns, you'll find a consistent time when you'd rather retreat and hide under the covers of your proverbial bed, when you'd rather collaborate and work with partners, and when you'd rather go solo to check things off your to-do list. Once you understand your own cycles, you'll be able to schedule your work to be more effective when it works for you.

What separates this book from the others, is that all that healing and alignment you foster through energy work and identifying your intuitive gifts, you get to apply FOR REAL in your everyday life, at home and at work.

Cultivate that life in leadership

You'll learn the difference between a leader and a conscious leader. A leader can learn all of the work rules necessary, they can recruit, they can hire, they can manage. But a conscious leader inspires. They work with the energy around them to align initiatives with spirit. They see the best in others and partner and support, even when it doesn't serve them directly.

Energetic and conscious leadership can look like starting your work meetings by reflecting on individual and team successes (a gratitude practice), drinking water throughout the day as the easiest way to ground when you're stuck indoors, or scheduling meetings for the week (or days) that you're feeling most creative (and not just because there's an empty spot on your calendar).

You'll cultivate your intuition at work by writing simple affirmations for yourself and save them on your phone screen and your desktop. Light a candle with a scent that reminds you of calm, success, peace, or any needed energy boost as you see fit. If you feel like you need a little extra dose of love, carry a rose quartz palm stone in your pocket to fidget with throughout the day.

You'll bring magic in simple and practical ways whenever possible.

Taking accountability for your own mindset, creating a safe haven in your everyday life, and surrounding yourself with others who support that mindset, even amongst the chaos, will bring you the extra dose of peace you need to quiet the noise. And when all else fails - breathe.

So why TF should you listen to me? Probably because I AM you. I'm a long time overachiever, certification collector, professional company ladder climber, and now... corporate drop out.

I worked really hard for a really long time to achieve a bunch of fancy letters after my last name, only to realize *they didn't fucking matter*.

I grew up with some intense intuitive gifts. I was seeing, talking, and listening to ghosts on the reg. But, surely, no one would ever take me seriously if I did anything remotely close to 'not normal'. So instead of embracing those gifts, I mustered through my teens angry, confused, hurt, and struggling. I shut it all off when I could (AKA ignored TF out of the gifts), and did what you're 'supposed' to do, according to whoever made us believe that it was better to be an adult than a kid.

So what happens when you do the "right thing", kill it at work, find something you like and are good at, put in 115%, have that pretty picket fence lifestyle, and all the sudden you're 30, you're burnt out, you're exhausted. So hidden, so.... fake. And then you have the startling realization that you have to do this another 35 years?

What happens when you realize that you're going to collapse. You have no choice but to explore your spiritual gifts to a meaningful level, but you also don't wanna be ALL IN on #spirituallife? I didn't wanna be a "weirdo". I didn't want to be so disconnected from the 'real world' and the real societal issues and run around talking about spirit all day. I genuinely loved and was REALLY GOOD at working with businesses and leaders to build better work communities and saw true value in bringing your full intuitive self to work. So how do you do both?

To make sense of this madness, in addition to livin' the corporate life, I started my own side gig mentoring others on how to be their full selves. How to practice practical magic. What I found was a ton of people that experienced true healing in all areas of life when they leaned into trust and their own experience. This little side-gig changed my life and forced me to hone in on my spiritual gifts.

Fast forward three years of living the in-between, I am a professional psychic medium, a spiritual mentor, an HR consultant, a business advisor, and a holistic wellness center owner. Still a lot of letters in and after my last name - and proud of it.

When you lean in, MAGIC happens. The stars align. Your gifts come out in droves in ALL of your endeavors; practical, magical, and a mix of both.

I'm Linds, and I normalize the afterlife and living a conscious life. I help executives and owners connect with their intuition without disconnecting to the real world to be more productive and impactful at work and at home. Let's help you balance consciousness in a corporate world.

HEAL

To know thyself, is to know others.

Chapter 1
My Story

This is a story of self-discovery, finding the right role, leading with passion and never settling for less. Just kidding, I definitely had to settle for less sometimes, but not for very long before I crawled out of my skin. Just let me be a little dramatic, ok?

I am obsessed with bridging the gap between the practical and the magical. I've played, and continue to play, a lot of roles in my life. It wasn't until a little "menty b" a while back that I was able to realize I didn't have to vacillate between all of these roles, and I could just be... Lindsay.

My entire life I struggled with being on 2 opposite ends of the 'reality' spectrum. I made my way through childhood thinking I was just really great at telling ghost stories. I didn't know that my ghostly experiences were any different than anyone else's. I just thought I weirdly landed in haunted houses and buildings and parking lots over and over and over again. I made my way through young adulthood and my teen years pretty angry, confused, silenced, and the OG emo kid. Not the late aughts 'swoopy bangs' one, but the skater, snowboarder, Green Day, Bright Eyes, Dashboard Confessional, Taking Back Sunday variety. If my mom let me have black nail polish, I would have rocked it every day.

I recreated myself over and over again. Emo, prep, grungy, smart kid, comedian, red hair, brown hair, glasses, contacts, you name it; I tried it. I never felt allowed to be my true self. Again - I didn't wanna be 'weird', and certainly didn't want to disappoint anyone (notably my parents). I had a bit of a unique family situation (a book for another day). But, I'll sum it up by saying that I had no idea who I was, and I wasn't really allowed to be anything other than 'the last chance for perfection.'

One day when I was 21, my best friend and I moseyed into the self-help section of a Barnes & Noble. She was looking for a specific book she needed for one of her undergrad classes. I was mostly looking forward to making fun of the book titles and those that thought they might actually be helped (oh, the Ego of an angry 21 yr old.) Tucked into one of the many piles of the B&N 6x6 flat displays laid a kelly green book that peeped out at me. Score - a dumb title. I aptly lifted up the book, put on my best sap face, sported a whiney voice and held it up to my buddy to read the title "WiLl I eVeR bE GoOd EnOuGh?!?!" As I kept giggling at my utmost wit, I flipped the book over and started glancing at the commentary on the back cover. My shit-eating grin quickly faded; as for the first time, I was reading a short passage that 100% described my life up to that point. Ut oh. *Insert foot in mouth*

I was connecting with something that I never understood before. I knew my life was a little different, but I never knew why. My best friend, always knowing me better than I knew myself, quickly reminded me not to be an idiot, and to buy the book.

In addition to many other life affirmations that I usually found in the pit of cynicism, this book led me to the three giant realizations.

- Only I have the power to change myself.
- Only I can set my own boundaries, and I can only operate within my own hula hoop of control.
- Once I understand the power of self and power of boundaries, I can master the art of influence.

In early adolescence my ability to influence manifested itself more in manipulation (Level: Expert). My childhood allowed me to develop a wonderful combination of intuition, emotional intelligence, and self-awareness which led to a career in managing people and processes. With a developing career in HR, I satisfied my need to manage other's behavior in order to manage myself. I needed to manage a process to move out of the subjective and into the objective. The problem with this, however, was that I was starting with others, instead of starting with myself.

As I stood in Barnes & Noble reading the back of that book, I realized that this was exactly what I needed. I took that book home, read it, and it changed my life.

That book gave me the very foundations for understanding my circumstances and understanding how I came to fit within and create [manifest] those very circumstances. It was an absolute key growth experience to understand first, that only I have the power to change myself, and eventually grow to the final realization that If I master myself, I can master the art of influence. What a powerful baseline to set as I formed my understanding for effective leadership! It's of no surprise to me that this lesson would be the foundation for the next 15 years of building a mentoring value set for my managers and executives. New leaders first have to understand who they are to understand how

6

to grow and influence their teams. Being a 'good' leader really has much less to do with understanding 'what' you do. It's much more so about understanding your team as individuals, as a group unit, and having a clear mission and vision to what you're trying to build in partnership.

I left that store without knowing the visit and stumbling on this book would redirect my entire future. I spent the next 5 years diving into my past, but all the while continuing to build what I thought was "supposed" to be my future.

As a kid, I knew my world was filled with spirit - walking around, sometimes interacting, sometimes not. You remember that scene in Sixth Sense where the kid winces when he passes the cemetery in the car? I get it. My family was very onboard with ghost stories, particularly my own personal ones, but I never really understood that my experience was any different than anyone else. I just thought I ended up in a lot of haunted places! Turns out, I was the one who was haunted. As I grew older, my experience turned from wonder and curiosity to terror and severe anxiety. Largely due to my Barnes & Noble trip and ensuing self-study and reflection, in my adult years, I've come to understand the "scary" years were much less about the energy around me, and so much more so about my environment and personal energy vibration. I spent many crucial years ignoring the signs and synchronicities that were pulling me towards my spiritual gifts and mediumship for the sake of that "normal" life:

Go to college

graduate

buy a house

get married

have a kid, and of course

work work work.

I built up QUITE the pretty little white picket fence lifestyle.

As you can imagine, you start to divide into a LOT of different roles when you have no idea who TF you are. The good news was that there weren't a whole lot of things I wasn't good at (turns out wearing masks is super easy for neurodivergent folks). The bad news was - I kept stacking up my "can do"s and "should do's" rather than my "my soul needs to's". Before I knew it I was exhausted, depressed, and burnt TF out.

The only thing that scooped me out of a deep years long depression, was my spiritual gifts SCREAMING at me to pay attention. The screams got to be so much that I couldn't continue to ignore them. So along with some trauma therapy, I sought out some spiritual teachers. If you would have told the wife, mom, and HR career professional then, that 10 years later she'd be a full-time professional medium & healer, own a holistic wellness center, and be helping executives and business owners how to live and build an aligned life, I would have cackled in your face.

In 2017, I made my first visit to Lily Dale - a spiritualist community established in western NY in the early 1800s. I'm a giant history nerd and LOVE the history of Lily Dale. My first experience with what I came to know as my own mediumship was from a Lily Dale registered medium. He forced me to read him, when I had no idea I was actually a medium. After prompting me ad nauseam to describe what I thought was a story I was making up in my head, I described an older man sitting at a kitchen table. After revealing more and more details, including what I was feeling in my body - chills, vibrations, temperature changes, you name it - the medium held up a picture to reveal the exact guy I had just described. As he knew, as an incredibly talented medium himself, this would convince me of something I never understood about myself. I could actually communicate with spirit. I was lucky enough to be a student of his over the coming years.

. . .

After a lifetime of confusion, depression, and an overall feeling of being lost, I started to come out the other side. With a new understanding of what energy was mine and what was somebody else's, I started to reflect on how I came to be where I was in life nearing 30.

Despite being totally unhinged, depressed, and hiding from myself - I questioned how I just 'knew' everything I needed to navigate my career with the success I had and why I was so great with my clients. The answer became abundantly clear through my understanding and practice of intuition. I was using my gifts all along; just not in the direct "let me talk to your dead people" kind of way.

As it turns out, I am a channeler. I spent my life and career tapped into every partner, client, boss, and direct report I ever had to completely understand them, their talents, and their gaps. Not because of, but in addition to channeling, I had the development and HR skills and experience to back up how to teach all my partners to improve for themselves.

I came to understand that it was my intuition that had led me to move from one position to another. I knew when it was time to go and time to grow. It was my intuition that told me to go back to school for my Masters (I hate school) for adult education. I loved training & development, but it wasn't something I'd really dove into at work until it was the right time to do so.

It was my intuition that brought me to a new company where I'd learn to grow an entire HR organization and get an inside look at how business strategy is interwoven with people strategy. It was through my intuition and influencing skills that I was able to form a crucial partnership and eventually friendship that would help me through the happiest and toughest of times in the corporate rat race. I traveled the country, I honed in my coaching skills, and I was able to develop a wonderful reputation as a "casual" professional - authentically myself. What a wild freakin' ride.

I knew the next step was healing and helping others on my same path. Although I was coming into the understanding that my gifts included communicating with spirit (and that they weren't just fun stories in my head), I was passionate about how to do that while also living a 'real' life! Being surrounded by other spiritual people - I saw how quickly you could lose touch with reality - and honestly that scared me. With my 25 year detour in the matrix building HR & business development and consultative experience, I knew I had to start my own company helping others bridge that gap between "woo woo" and the workplace. In 2021 I founded my first business.

. . .

I started my first company as an excuse to start using my psychic gifts with clients looking for transformational change in their business lives. What I found was I started attracting clients who had no interest in business, but just wanted a reading! It was (and continues to be) absolutely beyond my belief that anyone would ever find help and healing from me trusting and tapping into my gifts. My clients were seeking me out particularly because of my grounded experience in 'the real world' but the psychic connection for insights from 'beyond'.

Little did I know that as I aligned my work with my gifts, they would develop into the opening of a holistic wellness center, and eventually lead to my big exit as Corporate Dropout. I officially said SEE YA to the corporate world after 15 years of HR admin, management, and consulting to fully dive into entrepreneurial energetic and spiritual adventures. And now, we'll see what the future brings.

Whether we like it or not, we live in a corporately driven capitalistic world. When we combine our intuitive gifts with an understanding of navigating this chaotic world, we can truly build our own dream. My drive for all things is to normalize spirit and the afterlife. My original business tagline was to "bridge the gap between woo

woo and the workplace" and this still holds true in all of my businesses. HR work allows us to build conscious leaders and conscious organizations. My brand of spiritual development allows for the realization that you can explore your spirituality in a way that allows you to build a grounded life and not have to "go all in" if you don't want to. Mysticism is on a spectrum and my goal is to help you find your right spot in that spectrum. I help you become conscious in a corporate led world without losing what feels like your sanity.

One day I was deliberating with my business partner at my center about how to effectively market myself. (Sometimes the most frustrating part about being a coach is being incapable of coaching yourself). I was struggling to explain my mission in 'bridging the gap.'

"I just want to help people understand that they can be intentional, and mystical, and spiritual, but also walk in a boardroom and not be all like...." I stumbled and scrambled to find the words.

In all of her wit and wisdom she finished my sentence, "...and not show up in a witch hat."

YES! One thousand times, yes.

Chapter 2
Your Story

So what's your story, morning glory? Finding your spiritual landing zone is particularly difficult for women who are hell bent on showcasing their professionalism, but also going about it with authenticity. Wear the heels, but swear like a sailor. Burn the sage, but talk boardroom and business strategy. Talk to ghosts, but build a talent pipeline.

You can be both things, and still gain respect from your peers. My biggest struggle, not only in business, but in life in general, has also been my biggest strength: Showing up as authentically myself without fear of judgment. Being my intuitive self in the western world meant flying out of the broom closet, not being afraid to introduce myself as a psychic medium BEFORE diving into the consultant background. It's pretty funny, strange, or interesting to consider that although I've been a medium my entire life, I've hesitated to START with that description. I felt that I needed to lead with some credibility handed to me by universities and governing bodies - when it turns out I had what's made me successful all along.

While you may or may not be handling spirit communication as part of your intuitive gifts, you do need to understand what your unique gifts are, and how you can use them to benefit you at life and at work.

Here's a helpful introductory breakdown so you can start exploring your own gifts (along with popular tools to practice them.)

3 Physical Tools to Keep on your Desk

Pick one, or pick all three. Whichever one resonates, keep using it. There's no rules (besides the ones of the universe of course).

Tarot and oracle decks

You name it... any issue can be considered with the help of a divination card. Both tarot and oracle cards serve as powerful tools for self-reflection, guidance, and gaining insights into various aspects of your life, including work.

. . .

Tarot cards have been read (and played with) for centuries. The go-to Rider Waite style consists of 78 cards divided into the major and minor arcana. In the minor arcana, there are four suits and court cards, not much different than a regular deck of cards. The minor suits give insights into archetypes, influences, challenges, and victories. The major cards tell the story of life's big stepping stones and transformations (otherwise known as The Fool's Journey in the biz). They offer a structured framework for understanding the energies at play in any given time and can help you gain a broader perspective on work-related decisions, partnerships, and personal growth.

Oracle cards come in diverse themes and designs, often created by modern artists and intuitives. They are less structured than tarot cards and focus on providing guidance, inspiration, and intuitive nudges. Oracle cards can be a valuable resource for receiving gentle reminders, affirmations, and intuitive prompts specific to your work environment. They tap into your intuition and provide messages to support your work journey.

Are you Type A? Use tarot. Type B? Use oracle. If you're lookin to keep your intuitive tools low-key, there are tons of crowd-friendly oracle decks that don't look too "wooy". You can find them just about anywhere now, otherwise known as Affirmation cards.

Pendulums

Need a quick "yes", "no", "maybe"? Yeah, I thought so. If you're short on magic 8-balls, a pendulum is perfect.

Pretty much anything of weight hanging from a rope/chain/string/line can be a pendulum. Make it pretty, make it practical, or make it from a paperclip. You hold the string in one hand with the pendulum centered over your other palm. Slow your breathing and ask it to show you yes, no, and maybe over the palm of your other hand, you'll quickly find out the direction of your answers and use that for a quick answer when needed.

For example, my 'yes' is a clockwise circling motion. My 'no' is counterclockwise. My 'maybe' is a right to left straight line, or a dead stop. Yours could be completely different.

Test it a little bit with some easy questions - "Is my name...", "Do I live at [insert address]". I think you'll be pleasantly surprised at the accuracy! You might find that you start to understand a bit of personality with your pendulum as well - same with your tarot decks.

Crystals

They're pretty, they're decor, they're paperweights, but they are also BATTERIES filled with all kinds of intentional energetic goodness that serve whatever purpose you need at that time. Pick any crystal up and set it in your hand - you might even feel them heat up, cool down, or vibrate.

There are endless crystal types, but start with these for a successful workday:

- Clear Quartz; Focus, Clarity
- Amethyst; Chill the F out
- Black Tourmaline; Ground and keep the 'hounds' away
- Pyrite; Abundance & success
- Aventurine; Communication & strategy

The Clairsenses You Probably Don't Know You're Using

The what? Let's talk about clairs. Just like your real senses (seeing, hearing, feeling, tasting, smelling...) you also have clairsenses. Clair means 'clear', and a clairsense is an energetic and spiritual version of experiencing your other tangible body senses. These experiences are felt in your energy body, as opposed to your actual physical body. Every single human being has clairs. Some may be more developed than others. Some may choose to completely ignore them. Others are aware of them, work with them, and develop them. They're just like another muscle; you have to exercise them to make a difference for you.

Clairvoyance; Clear Seeing

You just got a flash visual of the moment you get your big award. You can picture your boss sitting down in a particular chair in the boardroom right now. You keep seeing little shadows on the other side of your office. Working on a new project, you can see exactly where to find a missing file.

These are all ways that your clairvoyance is serving you at work.

Clairvoyance is the intuitive gift of sight - this doesn't have to be right in front of you or "in the room". It can be in your mind's eye (and often is). It's often mistaken for imagination - the difference is that it's affirmed and validated later as truth.

19

. . .

And don't be surprised if it's not life changing - often the images are simple and symbolic.

Clairaudience; Clear hearing

You swore someone came into your office, because you can hear a conversation. But wait... no one is there. You have a big meeting coming up and you're so distracted by the ringing in your ear. Weird, though, it totally went away right before the meeting started.

Hearing when there's no physical manifestation of sound is the intuitive gift of hearing, clairaudience.

Did that song just start playing in your head and you automatically were inspired on a new project? Surprise - that's your intuition.

How do you know it's not just your ears? Listen, I love all things intuition, but if your ears won't stop ringing, go see a doc. If it happens suddenly, without any other symptoms, sporadically, and without any real interruption to your system, then you might consider it intuition. If it hurts or is a detriment to your day, it's NOT intuition.

Take care of your body! Without it, how could you practice your gifts?!

Claircognizance; Clear knowing

This is a fun one. When you "just know" with no other insights, intel, or hints, it might be clear knowing.

This is not to be mistaken for the ol' "I can just feel it..." that's another one coming up.

Claircognizance is like a download. It comes on suddenly, and it's proven through validation of the information from another source later on. It might be an insight from the past, about the present, or a hint about the future.

The thing about the future is it can be impacted in a split-second. It's fun to predict the future, but don't hang your hat on it. You can only control yourself and your decisions, not anyone else around you.

You might be hard pressed to be supported on an idea or proposal because you "just know". Find business reasons to support your 'knowing' and you're golden. To help you with this, I've included an activity in Chapter 5.

Clairsentience; Clear feeling

Ever get a 'random' physical sensation in your body? This is that "hair rises up on your arms" type thing. Chills, tingles, tightness, temperature... they will come and go quickly or sometimes even on demand.

Maybe immediately after you felt your back bugging you, you find out that your officemate is suffering from back issues. Maybe your phone rings and it's that one person you definitely don't want to hear from - before it even rings you get a headache.

If you're a leader - pay close attention to this. You might be able to open up a dialogue with your team to uncover something going on that's affecting their work, happiness, engagement, or performance. **Beware ADA - reach out to me for HR advice**

Now I'll say it again about the whole "my body hurts" thing. This one's tricky because it's a physical manifestation of a feeling in your body - that is NOT yours. This will come and go quickly, be unique to a particular situation, and often goes away immediately once discussed or validated. When in doubt, call a doc. Take care of yourself!

Clairgustance; Clear tasting & Clairalience; Clear smelling

These are not to be mistaken for the smelly kitchen in your office building (or your very own microwave). Clairalience is the gift of intuitive smell, and clairgustance is the gift of intuitive taste.

Ya know when you're just going about your day and you are reminded of Grandma's cookies? That might be Grandma saying hey. Both of these phantom smells & tastes will be unprompted, unannounced, and not tied to anything going on in your physical environment.

This one's not super useful for work, unless it inspires you to plan a wicked good lunch or happy hour. Or maybe you're a chef - in which case, freakin awesome. Meals and recipes from beyond. No one has to know (but it would be cool if they did).

Cheers.

. . .

Clairempathy; Clear emotion

This is very different from being a "sensitive person." Having clairempathy is not simply having deep feelings - it's actually being able to recognize that the feelings and emotions you're experiencing are not your own. This could be in the form of crying, excitement, anger, or joy (or any other emotion). Similar to the other clairs, it comes and goes quickly or on demand, and is not connected to your personal experience. Feeling super positive, then you find out that your bestie got a big promotion? Feeling cranky for no particular reason, and your partner comes in having a really rough day? You might have clairempathy.

If you do have clairempathy, it will be very important to work on identifying your own feelings versus others. Expressing or reacting to uncontrolled emotions can manifest in not-so-great ways at work. You could face blocks in success, issues with management, unfounded and ungrounded success, or confusion upon execution of tasks. *KNOW YA'SELF*

A real big pet peeve:

"I'm an empath."

. . .

Ok, Susan, are you really 'an empath' or are you just unable to navigate your body's nervous system in a healthy way?

In order to really be effective in identifying and practicing the 'clair' part of this gift, you have to first heal from your past trauma and conditioning with very real shadow work, and I'll often recommend therapy. Intuitive readings are not therapy. Psychics often are not also licensed professionals. They can provide healing, but seek professional help when needing to address your personal emotional experiences. To get started on shadow work, you'll learn more in Chapter 3.

Clairtangency; Clear touch

We're still talking about feelings here, except this time it's non-emotional. Clairtangency is the ability to physically touch an object and receive a vision, obtain information, or get inspired. Remember that old show "Medium"? How about "Ghost Whisperer"? They definitely rocked this gift.

Try not to break any physical boundaries here, but this could be incredibly helpful when you are working in another person's office space. Go back and check out Claircognizance - you can use the same activity here to identify how to make this information relevant to your business.

Understanding the various intuitive gifts will give you an idea of which you might experience, what you might experience as you grow in spirituality, and what might just be everyday life experience. Happy witchery!

The Importance of Meditation

This continues to be the most 'elusive' of topics for most exploring spiritual beings, especially those in business and leadership. The mere mention of the word and I hear "How, am I supposed to do that?" "But, I can't shut my brain off..." I know - I'm sorry. I was there too. I know the last thing you want to do is to be told to slow down and breathe. But, that's ok - contrary to popular belief, you don't really have to.

Meditation is the absence of judgment, not the absence of thought. The beginning of meditation is really a regular mindfulness practice. Practicing mindfulness can be as simple as taking a few moments to focus on your breath. Count the seconds as you breathe in. Count the seconds again as you breathe out. Rinse, and repeat. Finding your breath is just one example of a focal point for you to redirect your thoughts back to your meditative practice. It's ok to have thoughts, just remind yourself to return to your breath.

. . .

Entering a meditative state is the best way to make a connection to source and spirit. Think of it like you're a rechargeable battery and you need to reach your energy supply. More on this in Chapter 4.

Chapter 3
The Work

We're taking a bit of a detour away from work to cover an important topic. We're diving into Shadow Work. It's extremely personal, has a lot to do with our upbringing and conditioning as children. All of these things naturally lead to what kind of a worker and leader you are. But you can't truly be a conscious leader if you don't first know yourself.

I hope you weren't called into spirituality with promises of endless glimmers, incense filled rooms, pretty rocks, and sage bundles. This shit is HARD and ain't for the weak. You thought leading a team was hard? Wait 'til you try shadow work.

Ok, I hope that didn't scare you off. Finding and healing yourself is WERK, but it's also eye opening, and life changing to embark on your spiritual journey. Beyond the prettiness and freedom that can look like it is the spiritual life, is a call back to yourself. Before the conditioning, before the trauma, before the world got to you.

Your 'shadow' is a term coined by Carl Jung which is the unconscious side to your character or personality. It likely is something you don't really love about yourself. If you did love it... you'd probably be conscious of it! This is a little different than your ego. Your ego is something you are conscious of (and also might not love). Shadow work is essential to pulling up pieces of you that you might not be aware of, acknowledging them, understanding them, embracing them, and ultimately using the knowledge of that unconscious conditioning to better steer your ship. Remember, *to know thyself, is to know others*.

I break shadow work down into 4 steps; Identify; Recall; Reflect; and Release. I find this is the most beneficial way to reasonably and carefully lead yourself through this emotionally charged work. If done carelessly, shadow work can bring you to some difficult places. It's necessary to create an environment where you know you feel safe, supported, and comfortable as you work through some potentially difficult truths in finding yourself - without all the clutter and opinions of others in our lives. You might be surprised at where this work leads you. But ultimately, you'll come out the other end

29

feeling more in tune with who you are as a human, what you truly know is of the utmost importance in your life, and who you can rely on to truly become your highest and best self. The work is WERK. But it's so rewarding.

For each of the steps, you have access to worksheets to write down your thoughts and realizations. Each of these questions (and your answers) will guide you towards your next realization and understanding. You'll also find a great crystal to work with as you consider each of the questions and start to understand your shadow.

To access your worksheets, visit www.lindsaymastro.com/bookresources

Light a candle, grab a drink, take a deep breath, and dive in.

4 Steps to Knowing Yourself

Step 1: Identify

Crystal to work with: Moonstone

This stone is often light in color (white or clear and translucent) and helps to stabilize emotion. Hold it to your solar plexus (the space under your ribcage) to help with your emotional understanding.

Get ready to write. Use the included templates or any notebook. Go ahead... I give you permission to have ONE notebook that you will dedicate to your personal growth. Something you can keep handy in your day to day where you'll begin to note about all things shadow work.

Next time you feel icky - you're angry, you're frustrated, you're anxious, you're jealous, or things just generally feel a little undesirable - take a moment and let that feeling sit with you. You don't have to do anything else. Don't fix it, don't push it away, don't dismiss it. Just experience that feeling, and give it a name. The name can be whatever you want; it can be Red, it can be 7, it can be Frank, it could be Pillow. Whatever you feel like calling it, just name it, feel it, and write it down.

Take note of all of your senses in that moment:

- What do you see?
- What is the smell?
- What is the taste in your mouth?
- What are you touching?
- What do you hear?

. . .

Which of these senses aren't a part of your moment? Which are? Were any the cause?

As you experience these icky moments - repeat this process. Stay with it, call it something, and think about that present moment. Assign it a color - you'll use this for your personal trending. For example, my feeling of unease is red, and my feeling of sadness is dark blue.

Equally as important: Now repeat this same exercise with all of your good feelings. Some may find this harder than with the icky ones! Next time you feel joy, next time you feel love, next time you belly laugh. Give it a name, and take note of your senses in that moment. What color will you assign to this feeling? Example, my 'productive' is orange and my 'joy' is pink.

As you could imagine - there is no timeframe for this exercise. Nor will there be - for many opportunities for growth. Our growth is a lifelong journey. There will be ups and downs, but finding your shadow self will help you build on each experience and each emotion as you move forward day to day.

Step 2: Recall

. . .

Crystal to work with: Black Obsidian

This stone helps you find the deepest meaning in your shadow. If you look into it, you'll notice it reflects right back to you. What could be better than looking directly into your soul?

Now that you've identified and named your icky and joyful moments, you'll need to dig in to determine, at your core, what is the reason that you feel this way in these particular moments.

It's easy to say "I'm mad because she didn't listen" or "I'm so happy because he gave me a gift". But, I encourage you, with each answer, to keep asking "why" until you have an answer that comes back to you.

Here's an example of how your internal recall can go:

Why am I angry?

"She didn't listen."

Why didn't she listen?

"Because she was too busy on her phone."

Why was she busy on her phone?

"She was taking a break"

Why did she need a break?

"For all the same reasons I sometimes need a break."

Why does this make me angry?"

I just needed to talk, and when I don't feel heard, I am angry.

When are times in my past that I did not feel 'heard'?

The answer to this final question can be anything and everything. What you've done is turn a feeling into a reflection and an exploration into your past.

Don't feel like you have to, or even that you can do this recall in the moment you experience the feeling. It will probably be some time and after a lot of shadow work, that you will notice you actually do start having this internal dialogue in the moment.

. . .

Here's a secret: Once you do start moving from recollection to application of this work, that's when you'll notice your responses to the people around you are less a reaction in anger and frustration, and so much more in that of understanding and curiosity.

Remember when you named your feeling in Step 1? Next time you're feeling that same way, personify that emotion…. "Looks like this is Red…. what do I know about Red?" Revisit your notes from the recollection to find your answer… "When I don't feel heard, I am angry". This is the first part of your "I statement".

Step 3: Reflect

Crystal to work with: Selenite

My personal favorite! Selenite perfectly captures the light of the full moon to help ground you, and illuminate your truth. It will bring you positivity and allow you to start releasing your negative thoughts and embrace your shadow.

Now for the real challenge. We've reacted, we've identified our feeling, we've considered why we feel a particular way, and where it comes from deep down within us. Now's the hardest part - now we consider how to grow.

It's not up to anyone but you. It is wonderful when we have great support in building our best selves, but you are the only person who can identify who you want to be, and continue on your journey to self.

You can start this next step by thinking of an example that you used in Step 1 or Step 2. Ask yourself the following questions, and jot down your thoughts:

- What would you have done differently?
- How will you identify this feeling next time you feel it?
- Is the voice that's answering your dialogue kind?
- Is the voice yours? Someone else's?
- If it's someone else's, why are they kind, or why are they unkind?
- If the voice is yours, why are you being unkind?
- Review your I statements: Which of these are linked to specific events in your past?
- Revisit that past moment: Knowing what you do now about that interaction, tell your past self something kind. Give your past self some grace.

Step 4: Release

Crystal to work with: Rose Quartz

A beautiful and popular soft pink crystal brings you calm, peace, and eases stress, anxiety, and fear. When releasing old habits it can be a bit scary! The rose quartz aligns with the heart chakra, but you can place it near any area that you need the most love.

In order to make room for more growth, we have to rid ourselves of those thoughts, energies, and even tasks that no longer serve us.

You've identified behaviors in yourself that you'd like to change. You start to understand that you cannot control those around you, and you also cannot necessarily control your emotions, but you absolutely have the power to control your reactions.

For the situations you've worked through so far:

Make a list of the emotions, actions, or words that did not serve you well. For each of those items, identify 1 action you take to limit that situation moving forward. Use your I statements as a guide.

List 1 person who can support you in this; this support can be in any form; performing a task, lending their time, or even a simple conversation; you name it. Then ask them.

Next time you identify a familiar feeling, connect that to your I Statement, and take that 1 action.

Don't be fooled. This work is not a one-time deal. Anytime you feel stuck, triggered, confused, or disconnected, you can work your way through these exercises. These steps also perfectly correspond to the energies of the lunar cycle. We'll talk more about using those energies and manifestations in Part 2. Certainly, to properly manifest, you have to understand more about who truly you are to determine what exactly it is you need.

Let's Get Practical

To make sure you're actually doing the work, you can download printable worksheets at www.lindsaymastro. com/bookresources

Chapter 4
Intentional Living

What is an 'intention?' In the world according to Lindsay, it is a meaningful and prescribed declaration for the means of the action you're about to take. This action can be on any level. Some examples:

- A lifelong intention: I will live in alignment with my soul.
- A yearly intention: I will move throughout this year in search of peace & abundance.
- A daily intention: I will find gratitude in the hours I'm away from home today.
- A meeting intention: I will dedicate my attention to this group for the next 60 minutes.

Some intentions, unlike the above, are not time-bound. Setting intentions are the first step of any manifestation and also of any meditation. You want to set a clear goal for yourself. For this goal, you can skip the SMART stuff. Save that for the manifesting work itself.

So if intentions are set for an event, or a time period, then intentional living is the ongoing practice of putting intentions into most of your actions. Now, I don't want you to go overboard with this (enter: Spiritual psychosis). You don't need an intention for taking 3 steps from your kitchen table to your fridge. You don't need an intention for changing the channel from TruTV to HGTV. Most of life happens by chance and flow. The more you set your daily intentions, the more that flow moves towards those goals set. Don't drive yourself nuts.

Setting an intention is sometimes much simpler than it sounds. I think a lot of us expect a 'how-to', and quickly discover that we create our own models based on our own circumstances, experiences, and desire for change (ie... this entire book). However, it doesn't have to be a big complicated thing.

Setting an intention can be as simple as establishing a daily routine, a daily goal, a weekly/monthly goal, a focus word, or a few moments to reflect in gratitude.

. . .

Intentional practice is a cornerstone to maintaining your energetic transactions everyday. Energetic transactions = DOING THINGS; being human. I am a psychic medium. It's essential for myself and others, that I not only maintain my energy, but actually heighten it, in order to fully deliver messages that heal others. What is being a conscious leader, if not the desire and ability to grow and heal others?

Vibes

Before we dive into this GIANT topic of intentions, energy, and manifestation, you have to understand a bit about the vibe. What is a vibe? Well, other than that super aesthetic room you saw on Pinterest, it's also short for 'vibration'. That is, the vibration of energy particles and the frequency at which those particles vibrate. I'm NOT a scientist, although my life revolves around energy, so I'll keep this part brief.

We, human beings, ARE energy. Our physical bodies, our life's energy (Chi/Qi/Ki) and our spirit energy are separate energetic bodies constantly moving and shifting together to form our mental, physical, and spiritual experiences. We are not humans having a spiritual experience, we are spirits having a human experience. That is the default state of being. When we "become conscious" we're intentionally making our way from a mentally processed linear time bound life experience to a spiritually enlightened connected consciousness. This entire chapter will discuss the methods to intentionally explore that higher consciousness.

As a Spiritualist, I believe that life continues beyond the confines of the physical body. Simply put - ghosts are real. And not only are they real... but we ARE ghosts, trapped in a meat suit on this floating rock called Earth. When you start thinking of life and death in this way, it takes a lot of the spookiness out of mediumship, and makes it much more tangible to talk about psychic and intuitive gifts. Because - we are all (ghosts included) just energy vibrating and low and high frequencies.

Enter; the highly peeved phrase, "Positive Vibes Only". This is ignoring a giant portion of the human energetic experience, and avoiding the necessity to get uncomfortable and explore our shadow selves, in an effort to RAISE our frequencies. Negative vibes are not inherently "bad". They can be uncomfortable and traumatic. But they must be understood in order to become transmuted into more positive energy. So next time you want to grab that journal or tumbler plastered with "GOOD VIBES ONLY" just know you might be perpetuating a little toxic positivity (yuck).

Meditation & Mindfulness

Know what's different about me compared to other psychic mediums? I normalize the woo. I make magic achievable. Because we're all just normal people, who continually try to tap into our inner power and intuition. That's why we're here as sensitive beings! I spent way too long in the corporate realm watching regular everyday people turn into sycophants around the bigwigs. Guess what... the bigwigs are all just normies too (which will be of no shock to you when you ARE a "bigwig"). We're all just doing a really good job of pretending we're more powerful than others are. BIG ego trap.

My mission is to make mindfulness and meditation easy, approachable, and fit-able into your every day. When you make an attempt to practice this regularly, it's like muscle memory. You won't even have to try so hard and it will just become your normal. It's also a fast track from scarcity to abundance - those thoughts of lack won't even enter your brain, once you know how to be mindful.

Alright, let's be real - how many times has your mind felt like an insane street in Manhattan, filled with thoughts racing like cars. Honking, releasing exhaust, starting/stopping, slight fender benders... I know. Lots of people think mindfulness is about clearing the traffic jam. But really, it's about standing by the sidewalk and watching those cars pass by without jumping into the driver's seat.

"But, Linds, what's the difference then between mindfulness and meditation?" Did you know there is a difference? Kinda. They're two sides of the same coin, and they each bring their own groove to the table. Mindfulness is all about being present in your mind, fully aware of your thoughts and feelings without letting them send you on a fear-based spiral. That fear, by the way, is at the heart of scarcity and lack; those feelings of overwhelm and worry and need to control the outcome. Mindfulness pulls you out of the spiral and helps you see the bigger picture with clarity instead of anxiety.

Meditation, on the other hand, is like a focused workout for your brain. It's that sacred space where you dive deep into your mind's gym and strengthen your mental muscles.

Years ago I channeled the thought, "Meditation is not the absence of thought, it's the absence of judgment." It was after this that I truly was able to understand how and when to meditate.

· · ·

Here's the cool part – making mindfulness and meditation practical isn't actually as hard as you think it is. It's all about finding the rhythm that fits your life. You don't need to meditate for hours or become a zen master overnight. Start small, like with a 5-minute daily mindfulness moment or a 15-minute meditation session.

Everyone tells you to meditate, but no one tells you that meditation doesn't mean having to find 30 minutes of your own personal silence with legs criss-cross applesauce and hands resting thumb to middle finger on your knees. Meditation can be as simple as taking a few moments to focus on your breath. Count the seconds as you breathe in. Count the seconds again as you breathe out. Rinse, and repeat.

Meditation can be as easy as hopping in the shower and visualizing the day's yuck washing away and off your body down into the drain. It can be listening to your favorite music in the car on the way to work. It can be planting your annuals in your springtime garden. Your own version of meditation paired with an easy daily gratitude practice will do wonders for your energy.

The key to all this? Consistency. Think of it like an IV drip for your soul. Each of those little drips brings lasting healing and wholeness.

• • •

Remember those thoughts that used to make you feel like opportunities were scarce? (Used to, because now, you'll know better...) Well, with mindfulness, you're gaining control of those thoughts. You're no longer swept away by the scarcity storm; you're the calm in the center of it. And meditation? It's like planting seeds of abundance. It's creating that space where abundance can take root, grow, and flourish.

So, as you dive into this journey of mindfulness and meditation, remember: you're not aiming for perfection, you're aiming for progress. Each mindful breath, each moment of meditation - they're all steps toward an abundant mindset that radiates positivity into every corner of your life.

Getting Grateful AF

Ahh, the G-word; Gratitude. It's more than just a buzzword; it's a game-changer. Let's make it super practical and totally doable, because that's how we roll. Have you heard of giving AF? Quite the antithesis of its evil twin giving zero Fs.

I'd like to shift the perspective that you have to give "zero fucks" in order to lead a comfy life. How about just giving Fs about things that we already have that make us happy? I'm talking gratitude. Let's get GAF (#GraciousAF). Ever heard the saying, "Gratitude turns what we have into enough"? It's like a spotlight that reveals the beauty that already exists around us.

Gratitude doesn't mean ignoring challenges or pretending everything's perfect. It's about shifting your focus from what's lacking to what's present, and that's where abundant magic happens.

So, how do we make gratitude a part of our daily groove? Let's break it down:

Morning Ritual

Start your day smiling and giving AF.

Option 1: You wake up and grab your ph... NO YOU DON'T! Before you even reach to see what time it is, quick, think of 3 things you're grateful for. No pen, no paper, not even open eyes are required to start your day in an abundant mindset. (Question is... how long can you make that last?)

Option 2: As you sip your coffee or tea, jot down three things you're grateful for. It could be as simple as the sun shining or that cozy blanket you love. Want to make this a little fancy? Grab your favorite pen that glides just the way you like it and your GAF Journal (check out my favorite option on www.lindsaymastro.-com/bookresources). But any ol' journal will do.

Take a Gratitude Walk

During your walks or commutes, notice the beauty around you. It could be the vibrant flowers, the laughter of kids, the chirping birdies, the sun warming your cheeks, the bright reflection off the snow (can you tell I'm from Upstate NY?) or even a kind smile from a stranger. As you do, silently thank the universe for these moments.

Evening Ritual

An option for those reflectors out there. If you like to settle down before catching zzz's, open back up The GAF Journal and jot down the things that brought a smile to your face during the day. This practice not only ends your day on a positive note but also trains your mind to seek the good stuff.

As we get gracious AF, something magical happens. Remember those times when scarcity whispered that there's not enough? Well, gratitude turns up the volume on the abundance side. It's like switching from black and white to high def. You start noticing blessings that were always there but were overshadowed by the scarcity fog.

Your Gratitude Challenge

I dare you to dive headfirst into gratitude. Choose one of these practical tips and give it a spin. It might feel a bit strange at first, like breaking in a new pair of shoes. But trust me, as you take each step, you're stepping into a world of abundance and positivity.

Your gratitude practice can be doubled down in magic when you add in affirmations – those little power-packed statements that light up your mindset. Start with gratitude, add in some affirmations, and your world will be shifting before you know it.

The Power of Words

In the spiritual world, you'll hear a lot of gurus talking about the power of words. Change your words, and change your life. Have you heard of Dr. Masaru Emoto and his water experiment? He yelled nice words and mean words over some mason jars (ok, this is a classic Lindsay generalization) and the good water formed "perfect" ice crystals and the mean water formed "imperfect" ice crystals. You can find a more accurate and science-y breakdown in his book "The True Power of Water". But I need to give you that brief info to tell you these stories that I need to get off my chest.

Story one

Years ago, before I called him my husband, Mike and I brought a little beagle puppy into our lives. A super cute innocent looking little pup. We were so excited to "grow our family" for the first time.

A little about Mike. Mike's a metal head. He thinks he's a super tough Italian brute loud mouth, but under the facade he's actually a caring sensitive teddy bear in a Metallica t-shirt. Mike wanted this cute little beagly addition to our family, to aptly be named...

Killer.

I was about 19 at the time and my reaction to this idea went something like, 'OMG SURE THIS WILL ABSOLUTELY NEVER BE A PROBLEM!' A couple months after bringing Killer home (we really called him Killer B, B, BeeWee, Kew Bs... you know how they just gather new names).

50

. . .

Mike and I went to a family party. In conversation with my sister, some other party goers, and a very spiritually-driven family friend, our new puppy came up and of course his new name. The family friend gasped. She warned us of our misdoings and quickly explained Drs Emoto's water experiment. She told us how our bodies are mostly made of water. Due to this, according to his experiment, if we continually yell "bad words" over our bodies (like Killer), or to our bodies, we are essentially forming what would be 'tainted' DNA and 'imperfect' ice crystals in his body. This little pup would be imperfect and horrible since we named him such a thing. She surmised that we'd absolutely doomed our dog and his body and mind forever by naming him such a horrible name. Mike replied with more than a bit of a sarcastic banter about this horrible 'imperfect snowflake' experiment. Her finger wagged and her body shook and she cried for all of us. Mike, my sister, and I played along with the concern that our BeeWee would forever and henceforth have shitty snowflakes in his DNA. In case you're wondering, this felt like the real life equivalent of a forest witch cursing you and your family.

Flash forward 10 years later and I decided to do a deep dive into research on crystal energies. I signed up for a way-too-expensive crystal coach program (don't ask), and ordered the coach's big list of recommended books. I waited anxiously for the Amazon delivery and once it arrived, I excitedly opened up the box to see one in the stack: "The True Power of Water: Healing and Discovering Ourselves" by Dr. Masaru Emoto. It had one of my favorite things - colorful shiny pages in the middle. Much to my surprise, what did my eyes see? Perfect and imperfect snowflakes. Holy shit.

As I make my journey through all spiritually guided research, I come across the Emoto experiment and this rhetoric over and over again. Every single time it makes me laugh. Mike, myself, and my sister all still have a running joke about imperfect snowflakes.

Here's the thing... there's validity to the experiment. But people are missing the damn point! It's not the "words". It's about the intention behind those words.

If everytime I called my dog "Killer" I was yelling in aggression or accusation, I could understand why he was being a total dick. But if I'm like "Who's my good Killer B?! Who's my little buddy? Who needs a belly rubs?!" You think his cells are gonna form all "imperfectly" cause I threw the word Killer in there? Nah dude. I don't buy it.

The power of words is more about the intention of our words, not the words themselves. Words do have power, but only in certain context.

. . .

Story two

My parents weren't big 'swear'ers'. I'd hear the occasional "hell" or "damn", but not much of note considering the long family history of being raised in the coal mining towns of PA. I could count on one hand the number of times I'd heard "the F word" as a kid, and recall the stories in which I heard them. I don't know how I learned all the words I now know (and love), but I'll never forget the first time I used one.

I was in 2nd grade (you read that correct), in between classes, standing at my locker in the hallway with a friend. They told me something like 'DID YOU HEAR WHAT SHE SAID ABOUT YOU', trying to stir up a reaction. In an undeniably Lindsay kind of way, I looked up at them and exclaimed "I don't give a SHIT." And oh man. The minute the word vibrated off my lips, I was like YEP. That feels right. All other "ok" words were no longer strong enough to capture my emotion. 'I don't care' felt dismissive. 'Pay no mind' felt weirdly old ladyish. "I don't give a SHIT." Perfect. Having a consciously self-actualized moment at the age of 8 has to be pretty unique.

. . .

I knew... this is just something I do now. I also knew there was no way I could say that in front of anyone who would get me in trouble. Enter: A lesson in discernment. So off I went into life. Backpack and potty mouth in tow. Picking and choosing when I knew it was ok and not ok to use "bad" words.

Flash forward again... 30 years later. I have a terrible mouth, as witnessed by this book. But, I also don't use those words to hurt anyone, or anything, as much as I'm aware. So you can imagine when diving into spiritual woo-land, the conflict I must have within myself knowing this is just a part of me and has been for a very long time; Without influence, without conditioning. This thought that according to pop up gurus and faux-experts, my communication style of cursing, candor, and care; my way of uniquely and authentically expressing myself, "causes bad ice crystals" to all living things around me. Freaking devastating right?!

Like, how dare they?! Crushing my little sweary dreams all because they're confusing words with intent. So everytime I start getting down on myself for cursing while also being a healer and a spiritual being, and thinking I'm lacking; Everytime I edit myself because "someone won't like it" and it will be off putting to my audience; and everytime I change who I am just because an ignorant society says so, I remind myself that "I don't give a SHIT."

The moral of these stories is that words DO have power, but your intentions have more. Just because I had a dog named Killer, didn't make him a murderer. Just because I emphasize feelings with "bad words" doesn't make me any less of a healer. I propose this - change your INTENTIONS and change your life. Words have power, but only when you attach meaning to them. Words have power... kinda. Use your powers for good!

The Wonderful Weirdness of Affirmations

Woof. Admittedly, affirmations are the hardest part of my personal spiritual practice. But... I can attest that they've had a large impact that moves me closer towards an auto-abundant life. When I start to slack on them, my thoughts head back to scarcity wicked quick.

Affirmations are a daily dose of inspo. They unlock the power of self-talk, kick scarcity to the curb, and kick the door down to your own world of abundance.

Ghandi said, "Your beliefs become your thoughts, your thoughts become your words, your words become your actions, your actions become your habits, your habits become your values, your values become your destiny." But, Buddha said, "The mind is everything. What you think, you become", and that's much shorter and easier to digest.

Both these guys are talking about the essence of affirmations. They're like little power-packed statements that reshape your mindset. Repeat them enough, and they become your truth. This practice is not about fooling yourself; it's about rewiring your thoughts for abundance and success.

So, how do affirmations fit into our journey to healing? They are the bricks on the pathway from scarcity to abundance. The keystone to manifestation. Think of affirmative statements as your personal cheerleaders. Old scarcity beliefs are a lot like those wicked old photos in your camera roll - you took those pictures because they made an impression on you. They were your truth at one point. But eventually you forgot they existed, and now they stick around, take up all your phone memory, and you almost never go back in to delete them. Affirmations are your 'favorited' photos, and they're all about great memories and abundance. As you make them easily accessible, you repeatedly pull them up, and you're training your mind to automatically see these images in your head as your new reality.

Let's Get Practical

Personalize Your Affirmations

Create affirmations that resonate with you. They could be as simple as "I am deserving of abundance" or "Opportunities are everywhere." Phrase it as if it's already yours and it's always coming. One of my personal faves is, "I am abundant and money is always flowing towards me." (Grab that cash money babayyy...)

Say Them Loud and Proud

Double woof. This is the hardest part for most people. Get it out of your head and onto your lips! No, not a whisper... like, full blown convo. The reason for this? Sound is a more powerful vibration than a thought alone. Want more spiritual brownie points? Say it out loud 3 times. This... is my personal biggest challenge. Know that when you're struggling, I am too - we're in this weird world of affirmations together! Don't be shy; you're rewriting your narrative here!

Visual Reminders

. . .

Write your affirmations on sticky notes and place them where you'll see them often – on your mirror, your desk, or even as your phone wallpaper.

An Affirmation Challenge

Choose an affirmation that resonates with you or create your own. Say it out loud with conviction every morning, three times. And if that scarcity voice tries to sneak in, let your affirmation drown it out. You're the captain now.

Chapter 5
The Seven Chakras

CROWN
THIRD EYE
THROAT

HEART

SOLAR PLEXUS
SACRAL
ROOT

Our inner voices can convince us of some pretty crazy things. We think too much, we feel too little, and we tell ourselves stories based on only our own perceptions. We get pretty comfortable in our safe zone. In comfort, we rest, and while that's absolutely needed more times than not, it can lead to stagnation. That stagnation can be boredom, it can be self-doubt, it can be (and often is) rooted in fear.

When I find myself getting a little too caught up in stagnation, I think, "How would I work this through with a client?" Ahh.. there the answers come.

You might find this particularly helpful when you're caught in your own loop. As a leader, what would you tell your people to help them out of their self-doubt or confusion? What kind of advice would you give them, and where would you direct their attention? Are they feeling that strong self-doubt? You'd probably tell them their strengths, their accomplishments, and how they've pushed through these same situations before. Your chakras are like your own inner leader. They store historical information about our energy and tapping into that energy can help guide you through any 'stuck' situation.

When you feel stuck, it's often that energy isn't flowing through you in an ideal way. Your chakras, or energy centers, when 'unstuck' and wide open, allow for a healthy flow of energy. When you're in flow, you're having a great day. You're largely unbothered, and things seem to come easily. Each energy center governs a different area of life and activity.

. . .

Just like your own personal energy body, teams, organizations, and businesses also have an energetic blueprint. Being the conscious leader you are, I'm sure you've come across situations in your work where things are not flowing easily, and many things can 'take the blame'. It could be management (ut oh, is that you?), it could be the caliber of employees or business partners, it could be the customers, it could be the quality of the product or service, and it could be the lack of sales and revenue. There's so many directions to point the finger, but if you evaluate these issues through the lens of the chakra, you can identify how to heal the issue from the lens of meditation and mindfulness. I've got some energy related studies for you to prove it.

A Breakdown

Here's some red flags that you might start to see in yourself that give you the hint that your energy isn't in flow.

- You have to make a change, and that's a big NOPE from you
- Things are boring AF
- You're playing the comparison game
- You have some crap relationships that are taking a lot of your time and energy
- You're keepin' secrets
- You aren't seeing the big picture, and sure AF don't have a clear vision

- You feel a little untethered

You guessed it - each of these are tied to a kink in the energy hose that runs through your chakras from the tip of your head to the base of your spine. As you can imagine, it's a bit difficult to be consciously aware of your leadership, if you're feeling any of the above. Understanding and working with your chakras is foundational to your healing process. And much like shadow work - this is not a one time deal. When you're aware of your energetic dips and spikes in particular areas of your life or work, and start working with your energy centers, you're likely to be in a position to support others, knowing that you've first supported yourself.

There are many ways to address these red flags. You can listen to guided meditations particular to each chakra, you can recite affirmations that are particular to each blockage, or schedule an energy healing session to work through these blocks with some assistance. But, we're all about practicality. There are some steps you can take every day to DIY a little energy recalibration.

For reach of those above red flags, let's explore the chakras:

· · ·

It's a big NOPE to change: Root

If you feel extremely resistant to change, you're probably feeling unsafe or insecure about moving forward in a new direction. A fear of change, insecurity, instability, or general frustration is the dark side of your root chakra - signs that you need some balance in this arena.

The root is associated with the Earth element and the color red. Connecting with nature, walking barefoot outside, wearing the color red, eating red foods, and holding red or black crystals like obsidian, black tourmaline, carnelian, or red jasper will help balance your root energy.

How root issues show up in an organization:

Leadership is not making decisions and avoiding taking risks. There is fear, insecurity, and a lack of grounding that needs to occur before progress can be made. Financial security and a sense of direction is often to blame.

A study by the Harvard Business Review found that practicing mindfulness improved participants' decision-making ability by reducing the impact of emotional biases on their choices.

. . .

You're bored: Sacral

You're stuck. And being stuck can look like different things to different people. Sometimes it's difficult to get out of bed, get off the couch, or shut down the TikTok doom scroll. For others it means you can't get out of your own head. You're overly emotional, or you feel absolutely numb. Maybe you're not feeling very frisky in the bedroom, and your creativity is just absolutely shot. These are all signs that you need to check in with your Sacral.

The sacral is associated with the water element. Take a shower or bath, find a swimming pool, find a dinner cruise, or head to the beach. Get in or near the water. Orange is the sacral's color, so you can wear orange clothing or jewelry, eat some carrots or oranges, or get cozy with tigers eye, orange calcite, or sunstone.

How sacral issues show up in an organization:

This shows up as guilt, shame, and self-doubt. You'll see a reluctance to take on a new challenge, and a failure to create or build relationships. In general, workplace relationships suffer.

. . .

A study by the University of Michigan found that mindfulness training improved participants' ability to regulate their emotions, leading to better workplace relationships and increased job satisfaction.

You're playing the 'better than' game: Solar plexus

Your solar plexus is like your body's battery. When it's not powered up, your self-esteem can take a dive, your decision making is way out of whack, and you can feel straight up angry seemingly out of nowhere. You might be comparing yourself to anyone else rather than leaning into your strengths and unique skills.

For everyday balancing techniques, eat some bananas, turmeric, corn, or pineapple to incorporate some yellow into your life. Ever hear the phrase "the fire in your belly"? Your solar plexus is located right in your belly and associated with the fire element. Light a fire in your backyard or fireplace in the evening, and spend your day out in the sun.

How solar plexus issues show up in an organization:

. . .

This shows up as low self-esteem and an overall lack of confidence. Leaders aren't taking charge, and there's mismanagement and misguided teams and employees.

Your relationships kind of suck right now: Heart

This one's pretty easy to tell - your heart isn't in it. You're unhappy, you feel unloved. You are run by fear (love's opponent). Maybe you're feeling jealous, you're grieving, or self-deprecating. Maybe it feels hard to breathe.

The heart is associated with the air element - this is why things might feel a bit heavy. Breathe deep, sit outside on a windy day, drive fast with the window down (I mean... safely, but you get it). Heart actually has 2 color associations; green is correlated to more physical health related heart concerns while pink is associated with more energetic or spiritual health. Veggies are a great meal when you're feeling lacking in the love department. Surround yourself with rose quartz, jade, or aventurine.

How this shows up in an organization:

The organization might be experiencing isolation, loneliness, creating silos, and difficulty forming connections.   This can be improved by building relationships with partners and team members.

A study by the Journal of Occupational Health Psychology found that employees who practiced mindfulness had higher levels of job satisfaction and were less likely to experience burnout.

You're keepin' your mouth shut: Throat

You're having trouble saying things out loud and speaking your truth.   Typical signs that your throat chakra could use some healing is that you are quiet, not speaking your mind, hiding the truth, or keeping secrets. You could be fearful of being judged, being misunderstood, or generally having difficulty coming to terms with your own truth.

As we move up into the upper chakras of the energy body, the throat chakra is the first associated with the spirit element (we've covered earth, water, fire, and air). Your throat is healed with blue. You guessed it - eat some blueberries and grab some sodalite or lapis lazuli to help balance your throat chakra. The best way (and sometimes the hardest way) to heal your throat chakra is to SPEAK YOUR TRUTH. Easier said than done, and it's typically following a longer process of therapies and healing modalities, but this is the best way to a quick unblocking.

How this shows up in an organization:

There is difficulty in marketing or expressing the true benefits of the organization. There is a fear of judgment and lack of communication skills. This can be balanced by building communication channels, effective messaging, building rapport with partners, and appropriately influencing employees to support the cause through employee empowerment programs.

You've lost sight of things: Third eye

You're unfocused and can't see beyond what's in front of you. Maybe it's hard for you to predict what your future looks like, good, bad or indifferent. You're stuck in the present, or maybe fearing the worst. On the flip side, maybe you're living in fantasy land. Maybe you're not nearly involved enough in the here and now, have lost sight of your strategic vision, and have become ungrounded in your plans. Either way, you're out of balance.

. . .

Indigo is the color correlated to the third eye. Grapes, blackberries, and other purpley-foods will be a great way to bring some nutritional balance to you. Because we drift into dreamy visuals when we use our third eye, it's helpful to ground with some sunlight, keep your physical eyes open and journal what you see in the here and now, and sleep with some amethyst at your bedside.

How this shows up in an organization:

This is showcased by a lack of intuition, indecisiveness, and lack of foresight. There are unidentified trends, a struggle to make strategic decisions, or plan for the future.

A study by the University of Washington found that participants who practiced mindfulness showed a 28% improvement in their ability to focus and a 20% improvement in their memory recall compared to a control group.

You're untethered: Crown

When you feel totally removed from your goals, unsure how to reach them, uninspired, or distressed, you can bet that your crown isn't working to its full potential.

. . .

The crown is your connection to the greater universal spirit. It's what will represent your whole spiritual self. The best solution to balance your crown will be to meditate, pray, cast spells, recite affirmations - whatever words or practice you use that allows you to connect with the universal source, god, or energy that you closely identify with. White and violet are the colors you can use to help aid in crown energies, so clear quartz is the perfect stone to use when practicing self-reflection and spiritual growth.

How this shows up in an organization:

The organization is experiencing a spiritual disconnection, lack of purpose, and lack of vision. There are no clear goals and a lack of focus. Employees are leaving because they're not fulfilled and are not sure of their place in the organization or how they can contribute to success.

A study by the National Institute for Occupational Safety and Health found that practicing mindfulness meditation at work for just 25 minutes a day, three days a week, led to a significant reduction in employee stress levels.

These blockages described can be identified through only a brief observation of behavior and results. Once you have a general knowledge of energies tied to each chakra, you're able to pinpoint where healing and solutions are needed the most. Of all the above observations, they were not found by jumping into a meditation, channeling guides, or any of that fun intuitive stuff. It was just an initial observation.

Once you have an idea of how to identify your own energy imbalances, you'll be able to understand how these might affect your leadership, your team, and ultimately your organization.

Step 1 to healing your organization is understanding yourself. *To know thyself is to know others.* It's a long road, but it's one worth driving on with the windows down and the volume up.

Awareness and knowledge is so important to healing. There are endless modalities to subscribe by. Choosing a few to start with will give you the head start you need to heal yourself, your team, and your work. This is what I love about energy work when working with business professionals. You don't have to get all "woo-ey" to understand where transformative change needs to occur (but it's fun when you do!)

· · ·

The cool part of being a professional medium and energy channeler is that on top of the knowledge of change (which is such a giant part of transformation), I can assist that transformation through the communication with and manipulation of energy in the biofield. In understanding both worlds, I help my clients apply these energetic principles to not only their immediate experience but towards realizing change in their personal life, professional life, and in their organizations. Healing happens first, before transformation can take place.

Let's Get Practical

CROWN — AWARENESS, INTELLIGENCE / GROWTH, LEARNING

THIRD EYE — INTUITION, IMAGINATION / FUTURE GOALS

THROAT — COMMUNICATION & EXPRESSION / BRANDING, MARKETING

HEART — LOVE, HEALING, COMMUNITY / CULTURE, CHARITY

SOLAR PLEXUS — JOY, LAUGHTER, CONFIDENCE / TEAM GOALS

SACRAL — PLEASURE, CREATIVITY / CONTENT CREATION

ROOT — STABILITY, IDENTITY, GROUNDING / FINANCIAL

Ever get a really great idea at work, but don't have a whole lot of data to back up why it's a great idea? The thing is... you just know it will work. But you can't just walk in to your boss's DMs being like "Hey... I just got a feeling this is gonna be good."

I've got a great way you can use your intuition and tie your intuitive hit to a business proposal. You'll consider your idea, build out the vision of the idea in action, and use meditation to feel where this lives in your body. Based on your energy center, you'll find business alignment to start developing your idea from a business lens.

Here's how:

1. You get an intuitive hit with a great new idea (a download, a lightbulb, a message)
2. Find a few minutes to be undisturbed. Hold a visionary session with yourself (a meditation, a quiet moment, stillness, awareness)
3. In your stillness, take a few deep breaths until you're comfortable and focusing on your breathing
4. In your mind's eye, create a vision of your plan/idea in action.
5. Use the chakra map to find out the energy center, the emotional alignment, and which area

of business you're most likely to tie this feeling to a very real tangible business initiative.

When creating your vision take note of the following:

- What does it look like?
- Who's there?
- What are the sounds?
- What colors do you see?
- What emotional feelings do you get?
- What physical feelings come up, and where do you feel them?
- Pay close attention to where you feel this scene in your body.

Example: That Heart centered feeling - you'll likely be able to tie this idea to a culture or community initiative. How can this idea benefit the company culture or community? What kind of return will you get for that? It doesn't have to be directly monetary to find a return - it can be something like employee retention, which does translate to saved overhead.

Use this map whenever your passion takes you to undiscovered places. Don't let your dreams stop because you don't have immediate data. Start with vision, back it up with numbers, and you're on your way to some

AMAZING intuitive innovation, not only aligned with you, but aligned with your work.

ALIGN & CULTIVATE

There are so many levels of consideration when you're in the working world, and you start feeling like you might want a change - or to straight up get out of it. And to double the fun, when you're a leader, you're not only worried about your own future, but the future of all those that report to you. Happiness and alignment can mean staying put, it can mean exploring new opportunities, it can mean quiet quitting, or it can mean a more loud quitting *insert grimacing face here*.

The important takeaway here is that your aligned path forward doesn't always mean getting out and starting your own business. Sometimes it means finding the right spot within your org, or within another. Other times it means finding more opportunities within your same position. No matter what it is, it's always the unknown, which can be way more spooky-scary than ghosts.

The key to getting through this unknown and shifty period is to align yourself with your own personal mission vision and value set for your life and career. Once you have a handle on your intentions, you'll easily start flowing into manifesting your dream life. Manifesting works for your personal, professional life, and business life. I'm going to show you how to manifest, and how to use the lunar cycles for an extra umph! (Plus, who doesn't love staring at the moon?) We'll dive into some of my own personal stories and strategies of authentic and conscious leadership throughout Part 2 that you will find entertaining, thought provoking, and practical, regardless of your role as a leader in your professional life or business.

Chapter 6
Making Shit Happen

Before you can design your days and make all your dreams come true, you have to understand the importance of a manifestation cycle. "I'm manifesting my dream life!" has become quite the collection of buzzwords, that I'm sure you've seen pasted across your facebook and instagram feeds. But, manifesting is so much more than a wish and a prayer. I blame Disney for leaving the rest of the hard work off after wishing upon a star.

Manifestation requires a wish, action steps, celebrations, a 'if it happens it happens' type attitude, and most of all... a plan. To help folks make sure they're doing all of these things and really manifesting their dreams, I developed the PARR method:

- Plan - Brainstorming only; an exploration of 1 big shift you'd like to make happen
- Act - You'll dive into some action steps in order to make that change
- Receive - You'll celebrate your strength, progress, and accept those changes
- Reflect - All about appreciation and pivots

Manifesting is like creating SMART goals, but on magical steroids (and way more fun). You must have a well thought out executable plan, which includes a mission, a values alignment, steps to success, a support network, and a reflection and necessary adjustment period. This is always the weirdest part... Do all the work, then FORGET about it. This part is incredibly important, and part of the final release process (more on that later).

The PARR Method

Plan

In the first step in the PARR manifestation process; you make a plan for your big goal and focus on your why. You spend some time thinking about what it's going to take to work through the obstacles, and how to celebrate the little achievements along the way. You write down some real action you can take to move you towards success. Here's some questions to think about and answer for yourself as consider your next area of growth:

- Pick one change you'd like to make.
- What is working for you right now?
- What is not working for you right now?
- What is working for others right now?
- What is not working for others right now?

Reminders:

- You're not in control of other people's reactions. You're only in control of *your* actions.
- Others are only responsible for their own changes, and you're only responsible for yours.
- Is what's working for both you and others the same? Are they different?
- Are you truly looking to make this change for yourself, or for others?
- What do you love that you want to stay the same?
- Who do you feel is your support (relative, friend, community?)
- How will you know you achieved your goal?
- How will you celebrate it?

Act

In the Act phase, you DO THE THINGS. Here's some questions to answer for yourself and a mission to make sure you're making progress towards your desired change:

What are 2 things you can do to move towards a change, and what do you need in order to take those actions? Do it.

- Do you need more time?
- Do you need more help?
- Are you able to ask for help?
- Are you able to say no?

What are 2 things you can do to keep practicing something you love, and what help do you need to continue doing them? Do them.

- Do you need more time?
- Do you need more help?
- Are you able to ask for help?
- Are you able to say no?

Tell 1 support person about your new goal and what you want to do to achieve it.

Receive

The Receive phase is when you slow down a bit to smell the roses, and look at how far you've already come.

- Accept gratitude, abundance, failures and criticisms.
- What praise have you received? What did you do to receive that praise?
- Have you praised yourself?
- What criticisms have you received? What was perceived to have created that criticism?
- Have you criticized yourself?

Create 3 affirmations. Repeat daily.

Reflect

In the last phase, you take a look back at all of your work, and re-evaluate if any adjustments are needed, or if you're ready to leave the rest to the universe.

- What realizations have you had throughout your process?
- What other changes will you make?
- What are you grateful for in yourself?
- What are you grateful for in others?
- Who are your people that supported you to meet this goal?
- Who didn't support it? Who do you need to let go?

Write 1 a-ha moment

Where were you then, where are you now?   Journal about it.

Now that you know how to manifest with the best, now you just have to decide what you actually want to work on for yourself. Easy peasy, right? Wrong. I know you have a ton of different things up in that brain of yours that you're just dying to grow and make a positive impact. Don't put too many irons in the fire (like I tend to do). One easy way to choose what's in the highest and best for you, is to use your intuitive tools! My personal favorite tool is tarot for working out my next big area of focus. You can also do a meditation seeking answers from your higher self, or write down some options on a piece of paper and use your pendulum to help you make a decision.

. . .

All those career and leadership goals you have? You can ditch your SMART Goal development sheet and work through this process, just as well. What I like about the "timely" part of this approach is that you're actually implementing and developing a goal for yourself in a timeframe that inherently is realistic. You're not trying to spread yourself too thin to make a deadline that's on someone else's timeline. This is all about you babe.

Whichever method you choose (or lack of method), you have access to a printable version of a worksheet for you to use as a guide as you plan out your next big manifestation. Find it at www.lindsaymastro.com/bookresources.

Why this Works

Science, baby! In the realm of personal development, the concept of manifestation has gained significant attention in the recent new-age and spiritual boom. Many will claim that by focusing their thoughts and intentions on their desires, they can bring those desires into reality. While this sounds great at an esoteric level, there are more than a few psychological theories and studies that offer insights into why manifestation actually works. If you're reading this book, chances are you are as interested in the proof as you are in the pudding.

. . .

Dr. Carol Dweck, a psychologist, professor, and researcher, conducted groundbreaking research on how beliefs about one's abilities can influence outcomes. Dweck developed the terms 'growth mindset' and 'fixed mindset'. Her work and studies theorizes that having a growth mindset means that you have the belief that you can change, grow, and develop your abilities and intelligence. This can be done largely through effort, learning, and perseverance. It's no mistake that my PARR model includes all three;

Plan = Learning

Act = Effort, and

Reflect = Perseverance

Alternatively, those with a fixed mindset believe that their qualities are set in stone, and cannot be changed.

Henry Ford said "Whether you think you can, or you think you can't – you're right." Sounds like he was onto something.

Dweck's explanation of the growth mindset includes that regardless of individuals' various talents and aptitudes, every person is capable of growth through exercise and belief. Her theory proved that with the belief that you are capable of change, you will change.

. . .

Another study worth exploring is the phenomenon of self-fulfilling prophecy. Similar to Dweck's work, Rosenthal and Jacobson's "Pygmalion in the Classroom" study highlights how beliefs can impact performance. In this study, teachers were told that certain students were expected to have significant academic growth, regardless of their actual abilities. As a result, these students showed greater progress compared to their peers. Sounds a bit like our Dr. Emoto water thing, huh?

This study holds relevance for manifestation because it showed that the beliefs held about potential and expected outcomes can influence efforts and actions. When you truly believe in the achievement of your desires, your behavior aligns with that belief, increasing the likelihood of success.

Martin Seligman pioneered research into Negativity Bias and Positive Psychology. Negativity bias refers to people's tendency to pay more attention to the not so good stuff than the good stuff (ugh, WHY?!). Once, a long time ago, this was a great survival mechanism, but now that we're all in this giant rat race, our biggest threat is no longer the giant cat that's trying to eat us, and the same chemical reaction is caused by too many incoming emails. Positive psychology focuses on cultivating strengths, virtues, and happiness.

. . .

In the context of manifestation, understanding negativity bias gives us a great reminder to intentionally shift focus towards positive thoughts and outcomes. In doing so, we counteract the innate tendency to dwell on negatives. Positive psychology techniques like practicing gratitude and visualization (sound familiar?), align with the principles of manifestation, enhancing your ability to make your dreams come true.

The ingredients of growth mindset, self-fulfilling prophecy, negativity bias, and positive psychology collectively come together for a delicious recipe of successful manifestation. When you cultivate a growth mindset, you're more likely to set goals and continue working toward them. When you actively shift from a negative to a positive mindset, you're more likely to believe in your work and success. You channel your thoughts and intentions towards your desired state.

A Cautionary Tale

I went obsessively full boar into a reasonable plan to expand my HR consulting agency when I left corporate. On paper, I did all the right things. I recruited for a great team and found great talent. I marketed via paid and organic methods. I hired a sales and PR partner. My mistake was that I was operating under the misguidance that I needed to have a "legitimate" (read: 'not spiritual') source of income so I could live my life and spend my time doing what I REALLY loved: readings, writing, channeled strategy, and spiritual development.

Any income I did receive flowed in from all the stuff I really loved was immediately poured directly into the build of the "legitimate" HR business.. Some real high intelligence business math for you: Business income minus business expenses equals... no personal income.

So there I was embarking on my 2 years in the making, authentically aligned entrepreneurial journey, while unknowingly making a plan that resulted in complete inauthenticity and non-success.

Loaded up on a scarcity mindset, and riding another menty B, I was on the phone with my sales partner. I couldn't understand why we were doing all the right things with no success. As my head and words spun, she said "you need to stop."

Me: "Doing what?"

Her: "Everything. You're pushing this work making yourself crazy and when you're not doing anything at all, you're making money. Stop doing everything, and just be. Just exist."

Duh! I forgot my own advice. Make the plan, then FORGETABOUTIT. I totally distracted myself with what "should be" and not what was intuitively aligned for my gifts, my passion, and my business. I was obsessing about how the plan should be taking off, and spinning and spiraling on the lackluster results everyday. All the while - not pouring my anxiety and stress into what was working and what I truly wanted to spend my time doing.

It's a hard balance to strike - being aware, intentional, and strategic about making your plan for growth and success, and then trusting at the same time that the universe will have it unfold as it needs to. I stopped following my own proven manifestation method. Big whoopsie.

Hilariously, later in the same conversation with my partner, she was talking about a missing gap in her own business, someone to help write copy. In her own mini-spiral, she said "Wait... do you need a job?" We both cackled.. "Yeah, I need ALL THE JOBS." In one conversation I recognized the error of my manifesty ways. Minutes after I gave into just being and learning that I'd been trying to meet my own misaligned expectations, BOOM. Writing; an aligned opportunity for income.

The best manifestation for success comes when you least expect it, and when you FUGGEDABOUTIT.

The Importance of Letting Shit Go

This part is big. The last step of both manifestation and shadow work involve taking an inventory of actions and results, readjusting and preparing for any change, and then letting it dissolve out of your brain. You've made your moves, you've expanded yourself, but now it's time to release what no longer serves and leave the rest up to the universe.

You ever hear people say "as soon as I [cut this person out of my life] [off boarded that difficult client] [started living in alignment] everything just fell into place!" Yeah, me too. And it annoys the f*ck out of me. They make it sound so EASY. It's really not. It's super hard work to draw those hard and fast boundaries (and that's a whole other book). But, ya know what's even more annoying? They're right.

You already heard my story about trying to force misalignment in business. I wasn't letting go and going with the flow. I was holding onto something for the sake of what looked good on paper but not well in my soul. I didn't let go of what was no longer serving me - an HR focus.

Especially in the spiritual crowd, I hear this idea a lot. Discernment is IMO the most important tool you can develop as you embark on all things spiritual development. Call it being a psychic, or call it discernment, I can clearly differentiate the people that are truly abundant, healthy, and happy spiritually, emotionally and physically, and the ones who are making really poor decisions, banking on the universe to save them, and also driving headfirst into crisis.

The real ones don't have to talk about it too much, unless open and asked. They mean it, and they're living their best lives. They truly put in the hard work that's necessary to create an abundant life. The scary ones in this scenario are living so entrenched in the woo, don't take the needed action to move forward, and likely are participating in heavy spiritual bypassing.

I think my greatest challenge in life is and will continue to be balancing a spiritual and practical life. I can tell you that the more I slip into scarcity, the harder it is to live spiritually successful as a healer. It's a never ending journey - the spiritual path - and it's why I love supporting others on that same path.

Release, release, babies.

Chapter 7
Lunar Cycle & Personal Tracking

You want the moon?

Ahh, Ms. Moon. And so my love affair with Luna began. In endless songs, film, art, and fairy tales we see and hear about the beauty and the mystery of the moon. But, somehow the impact of the moon on the tides escaped me for many years. When I learned about the moon's impact on water?! Woah. And we're made up of mostly water? Could that mean... that the moon affects... US?? Double woah.

It's Just a Phase

Moon (lunar) phases are what we physically see (or don't see) each night based on the position of the Earth, the Moon, and the Sun. What we see is an illumination of the Moon's surface from the light of the Sun.

Each moon cycle lasts 29.5 days - this means it takes the Moon 29.5 days to circle once around the Earth. The Sun illuminates the Moon in a different position relative to Earth each night - taking us through all four quarters of the cycle.

This is a not so fancy way of explaining that each month (give or take), the moon will make one full cycle around the Earth, going through four quarters, or eight phases, of visibility for us:

- New moon: Only the back side (our invisible side) is illuminated; we only 'see' the moon's shadow
- Waxing crescent: The 1st crescent curve is visible, with majority Moon shadow
- First quarter moon: One full quarter of the moon (1/2 of visible) is illuminated
- Waxing gibbous: Moving from one quarter to one half of our full visibility

- Full moon: One half of the moon is illuminated, resulting in a "full" moon for us
- Waning gibbous: The Moon's shadow reappears on the opposite side
- Third (last) quarter moon: the opposite full quarter of the moon (1/2 of visible) is illuminated
- Waning crescent: the sun is only left illuminating the last crescent of the visible moon

New means it's a new cycle. It's not illuminated, and therefore usually not visible to us.

When the moon is growing towards full illumination, it is called 'waxing'. When the moon is shrinking away from full illumination, it's called 'waning'. Full is pretty self explanatory - the illumination is full and beautiful and bright. The quarters - well I hope we don't have to revisit elementary level percentages and pie charts.

Each phase of the lunar cycle brings with it energy that can help us in our own growth journey. You can harness the energy of the four quarterly phases for yourself to meet your personal, professional, and business goals.

Lunar goals should be more focused on emotional and spiritual developmental practices. Solar goals are more like we're used to when we say the word "goal". Solar goals might be more like "Finish my book in 6 months", "Add 3 more clients to my book of business", or "Save $5000 for a down payment."

I wanted to provide some case studies for you to illustrate the manifestation and growth power of the lunar cycle. First study? Myself. I've used the lunar cycles to take myself from a place of trauma, confusion, self-doubt, fear and conspiracy, (much like the 21 year old you already met at Barnes and Noble) to a place of grounding, intention, prosperity, and authenticity with a good ol' dose of 'I'm freakin' great at this and no one is telling me otherwise.' The line between confidence and grandiosity can sometimes be thin.

Case Studies

Lindsay: Case Study

After 6 years in HR in small businesses and large businesses, I took on my corporate consulting job. I spent the next 4 years building my dream job. I climbed the corporate ladder, made amazing partnerships, took on project after project, expanded my skills, and had multiple promotions for all of my efforts. All of those things were great, but after an incredibly exhausting 4th year filled with travel (46 flights to be exact), I had enough understanding, experience, and respect in the organization to point out the gaps, and proactively develop a plan for progress. I put together a killer business case, got buy-in from my partners, and proposed the plan to the powers at be. Low and behold, they thought I was right, and about 3 months later, I was feelin pretty great in a brand new position that I was able to create for myself.

It was, however, short lived. *Cue dramatics* I secured this new gig in March 2020. I don't know if you remember what it was like then... but the world changed a bit. I was already working from home, so the COVID life didn't impact me a ton. But, the business was impacted. Our main customer was small business. Many of those were shutting down, and certainly weren't looking to maintain systems and consultative support. Just a few months into my dream gig, it was taken away from me. I was in shock. And this literally could not be a worse time.

My 7 year old kid was staring at a Chromebook on the coffee table 'learning' her way through virtual school. My husband was working out of the house - he was an essential retail "hero". From 5+ years of non stop work and pushing too far, my body was suffering from swollen ankles, raging migraines, and the mental burnout was REAL. This thing that took me YEARS to create, with every last ounce of my energy and excitement, was over. Just like that. I knew I had to change my life. It was at that moment that I had the thought, "I can't do this for another 35 years." My intuitive gifts had been screaming at me for the last 2 years, despite my attempts to shove them aside and work, work, work. But, in that moment I knew it was time to use my innate abilities for good.

I also knew that my life was the workplace. Not just for myself, but having a really in depth understanding of how the workplace affects the people in it and the people outside of it. How business impacts people, communities, and economies. Somehow, my gifts had to line up with this knowledge. I had no idea how or when this would all happen.

With my obsession with the moon, astrology, and my newfound love of the Tarot, I started formulating my own manifestation method to go along with the lunar cycles. Within 6 months, I was sharing this with friends and family. Within 1 year, I was opening a wellness center. Within 3 years, I quit my full time job to go all spirit, all the time. Woah.

Lydia & Kim: Case Studies

Lydia and Kim are both managers for similar teams in the same organization. They were kind enough to share their experience throughout the same lunar cycle. For both of them, it's a Tuesday morning and the moon is hanging out in a waxing crescent phase. It's just past the New Moon in Scorpio and it's October. The skies are the same, but their headspace is very different:

Kimberly is feeling motivated and wants to dive into work, but she's struggling to find the real push to take action and get something done. These past few months have been really tough. Each day seems to be a repeat of the last. One issue compounds another. Changes in her company are her only constant. Her team is stressed, and she's stressed. Her big focus for this year was to prioritize self-care so she could be a support for her team. It was to be the "Year of Kimberly!"

On January 1st she set a New Years Resolution and said she would be focusing on relaxing, recharging, and grounding. But now it's October and she can't pinpoint any time she has felt this way outside of her 2 vacations to the coast. She didn't prioritize time to slow down and think about how and when to make this happen for herself outside of these few trips. She didn't do any work to charge her emotional and energetic batteries, yet, her trigger gets pulled day in and day out.

Her energy spreads out like buckshot, with no real direction and little accuracy, but sure to create some damage. She can say she's hit some targets at work, but only a little, and without making any real impact. Her team is miserable, she's stressed, and she has certainly not made any headway in her personal goal of groundedness. She quickly loses her motivation, and keeps crisis-responding to the dumpster fire that is her email inbox.

Let's face it... none of us want to be Kimberly. Lydia on the other hand...

Lydia feels motivated, just as Kimberly did. She's spent the last few days quietly and thoughtfully dreaming up the next area of growth in her leadership position. Last month she determined she wanted to grow her emotional intelligence with her team and focus on authentically empathetic responses when her employees are experiencing personal issues. Her inbox dings and dings, but she takes a deep breath and prioritizes which requires her immediate response - she determines very few do. After spending the last month focusing and practicing the skills and scenarios she knew she'd need experience with, she's confident she can really make a difference and coach one of her employees to feel more confident and empowered at work. She's ready to hold the first of many needed conversations coming from a place of preparedness, confidence, and empowerment. Not only is she making a conscious effort to help her employee, but she's also addressing her own goal of growing and practicing her emotional intelligence. Her trigger is about to be pulled by yet another email, but this time her energy is directed like a bullet at one target, and she's only giving enough energy to the others as is required. She has a lot of demands, and a lot of targets, but when she's ready to address her employee with more needs, all of her energy is collected and propelled towards success.

The only difference between Kimberly and Lydia is an intentional month. Kimberly has no idea that if she spent the last 30 days intentionally operating around the energies of the lunar cycle that she might have been able to work towards her goal of self-care and grounding - even if it was for the first time. Lydia was acutely aware of the lunar phase these past 30 days. The new moon had just recently passed; Kimberly starts another cycle without zeroing in on her goals and intentions, and will likely continue to move haphazardly in many directions. Lydia has reflected on her last months growth, has taken time to think about how this will lead her into real action in the next week, and has surrounded herself with experience, resources, and support to successfully take on a new challenge in her leadership career. Lydia moves from the new moon, through the waxing crescent, into the first quarter moon, ready to let the active energy build and build into a full celebration during the full moon.

. . .

New moon: A time to plan

It's the new moon, and Lydia already is aware that it is a great time to set intentions for the upcoming lunar month. In the past few months, she's worked on enhancing her empathy response with her team. She spends the New moon and following few days to determine what she'd like to focus on for this next cycle. Now that she feels more confident in providing strong empathetic support, she's decided to see how her new skills might impact productivity results. Specifically, she wants to do more work into understanding grief and how that impacts the workplace. This will be her focus this next lunar month.

As the next week unfolds through the waxing crescent into the first quarter moon, she creates a plan for herself so that when the first quarter moon comes, she will be ready to take real tangible action to move towards her goal. She writes down her needed actions, tools, resources, and support she'll need to grow this next moon cycle.

Your mission: From the new moon into the first quarter, take some time to breath, plan, and build your own energy as the moon also gains in light and builds its own power.

. . .

Pick one intention (goal) you'd like to set for yourself to gain a better understanding of who you are and where your obstacles might lie. This should be an emotionally charged goal - one that really allows you to dig deep into making a transformational change. Think more along the lines of "releasing guilt", "setting boundaries", "practicing gratitude", or "practicing curiosity".

The first quarter: A time to act

The first quarter hits about 7 days later, and Lydia's ready to put her plan into action. She finds a leadership coaching group that offers a webinar on grief in the workplace. She signs up for a course they're offering in the next few weeks. She also attends one-on-ones with her team to ask how they're doing both at work and at home. She asks what they're struggling with and what their successes were this past month. She offers a listening ear, without giving immediate feedback. She wants to catalogue these conversations to reflect on their future performance reviews, and also to give herself some idea of where she might need to adjust her idea of productivity in their positions, given the struggles they're currently facing. These conversations will let her find some common threads amongst her team and determine what are strategic changes she can make in her team and in her org, versus what are some immediate levels of support she can give to those that are not in a great headspace.

Like Lydia, the first quarter into the full moon is a time where you can start to take action on those goals you set for yourself for the cycle. Put in the work here when the moon's energy is powerful and building towards the full moon when you'll fully illuminate.

Full moon: A time to receive

7 more days have passed and it's Lydia's favorite time of the lunar cycle - time to PARTY! Lydia knows how important it is to stop and smell the roses. The moon is super bright and illuminates the image of Lydia and what she's putting out into the universe. Luckily, she knows full moon energy well, and practices gratitude for her team, celebrates their accomplishments, acknowledges herself and her own actions taken to move herself and her team forward and soaks in all the good in life.

Lydia knows that if she puts out this optimism, it will come back to her in the most exciting of ways, with little effort.

．　．　．

Meanwhile, Kimberly's still unfocused, feels slighted at the inability to make this the 'year of Kimberly', and is *so* pissed about her inbox piling up. The moon's shining back on this energy too, but fizzles out while Kimberly can't see some of the bright options she might have ahead of her.

The full moon harnesses the energy you'll need for reflection. The full moon into the third quarter is a time when you should be gathering what you've created so far, celebrating your wins, and making positive changes.

Last quarter: A time to reflect

Kimberly is about 3 weeks into the month, and hasn't made much progress on her energy or her inbox. She didn't take time to plan how to make a big change in her head or in her physical space, and now another month is about to fall behind her and she's spent another month being unhappy about her situation and her team is feeling it.

Lydia's team is feeling inspired from the kudos they just received last week, is clear on their vision for the next month, and feel supported in the fact that when they do have some personal issues going on, they will be able to come to work, do what they're capable of, and know they have a leader who will support them in any case. Their productivity has increased because Lydia has prioritized time for her employees to reflect themselves and focus on their own intentions, personal or professional.

Lydia takes some time to write down her and her team's accomplishments. She revisits her plan she wrote down from the new moon, and sees if she's decided to skip over any actions, or taken any in addition to what she'd originally anticipated. She does a "start, stop, continue" exercise with her team to cut off any unneeded and unintentional tasks. She physically cleans out her workspace - she wants an uncluttered and grounded start to the next lunar cycle.

Lydia is confident in who she is, what she's accomplished, and proud that she's able to be a conscious intentional leader and build a conscious team. She becomes more excited about her values and who she is at her core. She's built in time to reflect on this, and get excited about more to come.

As the last quarter moves back into the next new moon, it is a time to reset and clear out the energy that no longer serves you to make room for the new exciting growth you'll experience in the next lunar round.

Let's Get Practical

I am a believer (and promoter) that we cannot truly realize success (personal or professional) unless we have identified who we are as individuals. *To know thyself, is to know others.*

Earlier in Chapter 3, we reviewed how shadow work coincides perfectly with the energies of the lunar cycle. As you work your way through each step of the work, you can pace yourself as follows:

- New Moon: Identify
- First Quarter: Recall
- Full Moon: Reflect
- Last Quarter: Release

A great way to track your feelings, moods, reactions, and growth over time is by simply tracking your day throughout each moon cycle. Some people do this by journaling (which I recommend over and over again!). But, if you are like me, you're a visual person, and you need something right in front of you that gives you an idea of how you're trending and what might be contributing to your thoughts and feelings.

• • •

Include details each day like how you slept, what activities you participated in, or for the ladies, even include your menstrual cycle (you might not be surprised to see that your cycle aligns directly with the phases of the moon). A few examples I like to include are how 'busy' work was, whether or not I grounded/meditated, exercised, or got busy (wink). Whatever is impacting your daily life that you feel could tie back to your physical and emotional feelings each day are all worth including.

To record your daily feelings, use the colors you've assigned from The Work; Step 1: Identify, or make a key for yourself to easily refer back to. Make sure to leave room for 2-4 feelings. For example, I might feel sad, but it doesn't mean I'm not motivated. I like to track happy vs sad, motivated vs stagnant, sick vs strong. I could be one of these 3 things each day and they don't depend on each other. However you like to record it, there's no rules. Make it your own.

For each day of each lunar cycle, track all your needed experiences to see how you progress through the cycle. Each lunar cycle is 29.5 days, or approximately one month. After you complete a full cycle, and a few thereafter, you'll be able to see if you typically feel a certain way during certain times of the lunar month.

. . .

Depending on your astrological birth chart, you might also recognize you feel certain ways at particular phases of the lunar cycle. For example, in general the Full Moon is a time to claim what's yours and make things happen (#manifestation). However... if around the Full Moon you've tracked that you typically feel drained, maybe hold off on those manifestations until you feel your most powerful! Mind the moon, but make it work for you!

Here's an example of a Personal Trending chart. To access a blank copy, find the printable at www.lindsaymastro.com/bookresources.

Lunar Tracking

Moon: __Snow Moon__

Month: **February - March**

Legend:
- Joyful, Silly
- Sad, Depressed
- Productive, Empowered
- Sick, Tired
- Calm, Peaceful
- Anxious, Angry
- Grounded
- Exercise
- ♡ Love
- R Ritual
- m Meditation

Moon phases:
- New Moon
- Waxing Crescent
- First Quarter
- Waxing Gibbous
- Full Moon
- Waning Gibbous
- Last Quarter
- Waning Crescent

113

Chapter 8

Do You Stay or Do You Go?

You picked up this book because you're a leader. You could be a manager in a corporate organization. You could be a business owner. Some of you may take on a leadership role at home, managing the ins and outs of family life. You want to know how to be more conscious in that chaotic, corporate world.

My journey to consciousness in corporate eventually led to my departure. But, I spent three years trying successfully to merge intuitive gifts and my work, and it led me to share that with you. Just because I eventually chose to leave, does not mean that will be your path. The soul path is not linear. There will be back and forth, give and take. Alignment is not always easy. There were days I wanted to throw in the towel, but I kept pushing forward. And when it was truly time to go, it was not in a burst of flames. I put my ducks in a row, I made my intuitively aligned career and business plan, I explored all options, and it just felt right. There were internal and external factors at play. But ultimately my decision was made when I knew I was in alignment.

Your alignment will look different - because we all have our own paths. When you choose to stay and bring consciousness into corporate, you learn to bring the entrepreneurial spirit to work. You turn a job into a career. You have your own personal mission and vision that you bring to your corporate environment, no matter how big or small. Most importantly, it might not be only working yourself through this process, you could be helping those on your team as well.

Quiet Quitting: A Viable Option?

Sometime in 2022 the term "Quiet Quitting" emerged. It was all the rage in the HR community. The term basically referred to workers staying in their jobs, but doing essentially the bare minimum. No passion. No drive. Just a location, a laptop, and a paycheck. Why was everyone bailing from the corporate world? And why were there also overnight experts coming out of the woodwork to preach on the topic? A year before I quit corporate, I had no idea I'd be doing it myself, and maybe not so quietly. However, I was well aware that I had 'quiet quit' years before when my pretty little corporate ladder broke under my feet. I poured every ounce of energy I had and more into creating my most perfect position, only for the economic landscape to take that away in an instant. I luckily (through my partnerships) was able to move quickly into a new position, but I never really got over the bitterness of losing everything I'd worked for.

Quiet quitting seems like a pretty solid strategy when you're burned out, more interested in spiritual stuff, and, well... pissed off. But, what happens when you're quiet runs out? What happens when you can't take it anymore, but you have no backup plan?

You create your backup plan.

My plan started in the late hours of 2020, when I decided to share my gifts with the world. The plan developed for over 2 years before it led me to the next big shift in life. Your plan, as I said before, does not have to involve the big quit. It can be staying put where you are, but with more excitement, appreciation, and passion for what it is you do, or will soon be doing.

So how will you create your plan? Why, through the manifestation process, of course!

Plan, act, receive, reflect.

. . .

Before you start your Plan phase and dive into a lunar cycle manifestation, you have a bit more work to do. This time, you're first going to create your mission, your vision, and your values statements. You have two choices; you can create one of these for your career alone, or you can create them for your life.

If you create your statements for career only, it will give you a basis for where to direct your wants and needs you're about to manifest. This is incredibly helpful and in no way is a bad thing to do. All gravy.

However, if you create one for your life, be prepared to make some serious career decisions in line with your life's mission & vision. This is a more 'serious' step to take in regard to your career. You'll have nowhere to hide when seeking out true holistic alignment for your work and your life. This is what I did when I knew something was broken. I refused to continue to act as two people, and my mission was to be authentic and open about my abilities.

As a first step, it's likely not realistic to say "This month I will completely revamp my career and no longer be two people!". That's not going to be my manifestation in one lunar cycle. It is realistic however to take one small goal that moves towards achieving that end state, and work on that for the lunar month. Coming out of the broom closet, for example, takes a hell of a lot of courage and tenacity. My first manifestation might be to become more transparent in my communications. That's absolutely something I can build towards in 29.5 days.

Curating Your Aligned Career

Here are some simple formulas to follow for creating your statements. Whether you're doing this in the scope of your career only, or your entire life, you can follow the same formula:

Your Mission Statement

Your mission is something you are determined to work on for the foreseeable future. This will be a reminder to yourself about your guiding light and focus and something you can tie objectives to. This may adjust and change later in time, but you should not change this until there is at least consistent practice and progress towards this goal.

The first mission statement you make should be personal. As you shift and change and feel fulfillment, you might make a change for more of a community impact.

. . .

A helpful formula to follow is below, but phrase any way you'd like. Make sure to include your intention, a high level action step, and a promised time frame.

I [*intention*]. [*Action and how you will achieve this*] on a [*timeframe*] basis.

Ex. I *will be a lifelong learner.* I *practice curiosity and seek understanding in topics that foster the spiritual and professional connection* on a *monthly* basis.

Your Vision Statement

Your vision statement is how you intend to see your mission pan out. Think big! This likely will not change as often as your mission statement does, but might still grow and shift. We like to keep it agile, because life can be unpredictable.

In [*time frame*] I will [*end state*] with [*support people*] by [*action taken*].

Ex. In *5 years* I will *be a successful intuitive leadership coach* with *support from a team of conscious leaders* by *sharing my gift of channeling with the world.*

. . .

Your Values

List 3-5 descriptive and guiding words that you will choose to reflect on daily. You can add these to your gratitude practice, and create affirmations.

As an example, my values are:

- *Authenticity*
- *Passion*
- *Curiosity*
- *Intuition*

In every decision I make, I revisit these guiding principles. I already know they are truly aligned with who I am as a person. I don't have to 're-evaluate' who I am with every new optional path that pops up in front of me. If I were to ask myself "Should I volunteer for this new project?"

Considerations:

- Does it allow me to remain authentic to myself and to my team?
- Is it something I'm passionate about, or does it lead to something I'm passionate about?
- Can I maintain curiosity surrounding the things that might not go well?
- When I tap into my energy source, how does it sit within my body? What am I feeling? Am I receiving any messages?

Based on that simple list, if I could answer yes, and didn't 'feel' weird about it. I would move forward with my decision. I do want to emphasize that even if I could say yes to all of these things. I would still evaluate the more tangible considerations, like timing, bandwidth, support structures, and other known environmental changes on the horizon. Be aware of your ability to say no, even when it doesn't 'feel' like you can.

You might notice that none of the above considerations have anything to do with money. I would strongly advise you to move in the direction of alignment and empowerment. The money will follow. My salary increased with every new step I took (other than the big quit). It might make your financially impacted partner happy to know you're about to rake in more cash, and certainly you too... but it was never the reason for a change. Just a happy impact!

Supporting your Employees through Big Changes

So the question is asked by leaders everywhere: What can we do about our employees quitting on us? When someone's made up their mind... not a whole lot. That's why it's important to be proactive about these conversations, support them where they're at and help them develop their own mission & vision. Opening up dialogue about development conversations creates a fair and equitable workplace and actively shows conscious leadership.

Employees should have a reasonable ability to create boundaries for themselves (ie, saying "no", but it doesn't give them an excuse to shirk their duties. There is likely going to be a realignment of expectation and output. Open communication is an absolute must to create a happy and productive workforce.

"How can I have a conversation as an employee with my leader about workload expectations?"

Gather data. Implement your own mini time study for a month to track the categories of work you are performing and the amount of time it takes you. Compare the results against your job description, expectations, or performance review for efficiencies, roadblocks, status quo. With this quantitative data, in addition to your qualitative feedback on culture, support, and work environment, a responsible leader will likely be able to immediately support some requests for change and make a larger impact to your team or organization.

"In what ways can a leader make sure an employee feels valued?"

Calendars: Give employees a break - they're humans. Let your employee structure their calendar how they see fit. If your employee is getting the job done with little to no mistakes, contributing to the work, and showing up in face time or in output, ask yourself how your performance expectations are aligned with the needs of the job itself.

Remote computer monitoring: Give explicit expectations of when and how programs are being reviewed. It should not be a surprise when you bring a screenshot to your employees. Better yet - lay off the monitoring unless it's specifically for service review purposes.

Performance Evaluations: We work because we have to, and hopefully also because we love it, but it's hard to find both. Check your recency bias at the door. "What have you done for me lately?" is for your relationship, not your employees.

Trust & Respect: Most employees want to do a good job. You can create the best culture in the world - it won't be for everyone. Help your employees find alignment with their passions, even if that means it's not on your team. Offer and foster open candid conversations about their day to day, whether it's a story about home or work. At the end of the day, as we're all finding in the post COVID world, it's all work-related and work-impacting.

"I'm pretty great with my leadership, I don't think I'm really impacted."

Assume you are. Do you have employees who traditionally raised their hand for projects and initiatives who no longer offer up their thoughts? Are you, yourself, no longer "all-in" for company wide initiatives that don't fit your value pattern? Is your team breezing over change without much conversation or complaint?

"How bad is quiet quitting for business?"

You might hear that turnover and productivity is impacted, but I would argue that you may have had inflated productivity previous to the massive burnout. The amount of effort that was put in previously was likely above and beyond the job requirements. Turnover won't be impacted when people are 'quiet quitting'. It's impacted later. Eventually quiet quitters will find alignment somewhere else, if you don't provide it where they're at. Right now, these people are sliding under the radar, and only concerned with what will get them in trouble, or noticed. Be concerned about your numbers 6 - 12 months from now, not in the moment. Make sure you're tracking your trending and having open conversations.

Innovation is really what suffers. There's little creativity and passion flowing when employees are unengaged and creativity and passion are prerequisites for innovation. Foster their mission, vision, and values, and their creativity will stick around.

"How do I bring this up with my employee?"

Ask them about it. Hold an open space for employees to talk about what quiet quitting means to them. Have they experienced it? What would make them feel valued? What would cause them to "quiet quit"? How do they like to structure their day? What's their favorite part of the job - and how can you foster more of that? What's their least favorite part of the job, why, and is there another employee on your team that's better fit for that requirement? If not, what support can you or the team offer that would make that feel less like a burden. What is the best day they've ever had at work and why was that the best day?

Acknowledge that you don't always need "more". Many times employees are putting this stress on themselves, and without acknowledging that all this great work they've delivered was above expectations, it quickly sets the new bar. Quit moving the goal post. Take a breather.

The Great Regret

After the 'blow up' of the Great Resignation and Quiet Quitting, came the settling of 'The Great Regret'. There was quite a bit of rhetoric I saw surfacing about 'The Great Regret', and a 'rebalancing of scales' as it related to job vacancy and a shift from an employee to an employer-led market. I have a sneaking suspicion that the generational trend (lookin at you Z'ers) found in this response had SO much to do with the blow up of the Coaching and online support industry - one with false promises of outrageous income for little work.

When massive layoffs occur, employees are more likely to jump ship to greener pastures. One that promises more stability and generally a better culture to spend day in and day out. Employees see the potential in another organization or in creating their own business. The number of employees leaving due to fear of a layoff or more work on their plate, shows up as a voluntary termination - which is a bit ironic. Something made them bounce. This 'data' makes some of the big corporate guys say, 'Ha! Told ya so! Grass isn't always greener, now we're back in control! Here they come flooding back!' But, that just wasn't true.

Turnover and vacancy is increasingly an issue, particularly in retail. I've seen some really successful entrepreneurs in the online space absolutely kill it outside their corporate roles. And others are finding those true leaders who made the shift and followed suit. As a business owner and leader, you might think the tides are turning in your favor when you read something like "The Great Regret" and you might think there's no need to be strategic, because they'll all 'come running back.'

Bottom line is, while data is helpful, it can also be used to paint a certain narrative. Have conversations with your team and people to meet them where they're at. There are solutions to move through the big Q, but only when you're listening to the right people; that includes that little voice in your head and feeling in your gut.

Loud Quitting: When it's Time to Go

You know already, my final decision was pulling my own personal corporate plug. I took some time to fully consider this giant decision. I had a very successful career, with a successful company, on an absolutely killer team, but it was just not right for years. Especially in the last few months, when the company direction started changing, I was well aware the company vision was no longer my vision. This misalignment was more than I could stomach, mostly due to a complete shift in values that no longer met my values. After months and MUCH deliberation and ongoing talks with my leader, I officially submitted my two weeks notice. Freakin YIKESSSS.

On my very last day, when I got the invite on my calendar for a "Farewell call" I wasn't sure how to feel. I felt free, but also so sad. I was terrified, but also so excited. Due to directional changes, our tight team was in turmoil, being ripped apart. Most of us were very close. For a team of 16, that was rare and unique. Most of us had known each other for a long time, if not in this position, then in a prior one. Truly a collection of extremely talented, funny, empowered, and productive professionals, all being ripped down to the studs. I'd never seen anything like it. Our leader was in the midst of pure chaos, and there was so much uncertainty and very little detail that, inevitably, people were assuming the worst and making up stories. I expected the call to be both great and awkward.

. . .

I could not have been more wrong.

It was lovely, and wonderful, and sad, and heartfelt. And difficult. The call put aside all of the craziness, and without any agenda or schedule, the team one by one shared a funny story, a note, a memory, a note of gratitude, or whatever else it was. It was almost like being at my own funeral. I tried to hold it together, but I was inconsolable. Not only were these people my coworkers, but my best and closest friends.

You spend the majority of your waking life at work, and when you work on a team like this, you know each other more than most. I loved this team. And I was REALLY struggling to leave it. I struggled to keep a list of some of the more important and resounding messages I took from the call that day.

A word I kept hearing in this meeting and for the few weeks prior was courage. When I announced my corporate departure, I had a lot of people say to me, "You are so courageous!", or "You're showing so much courage in what you're doing!" I never considered it that at all. Quitting my full time job, moving into entrepreneurship; I never considered it courageous. If anything, it feels a little irresponsible. And that's obviously my own conditioning. What the world (America anyways) wants us to think is; be stable, get an ongoing paycheck.

If it's courageous to quit, does that mean it's not courageous to stay? I don't think so. Sometimes the most courageous thing you can do is exactly what you need to, even when it's scary. Sometimes that means staying in your job and not leaving. It's courageous to live up to your highest potential - and that should dictate your decision to stay and grow, or go and grow.

Having courage in making your decision, whatever that might be, is making an intentional and soul-aligned choice for your career. Some people just quit because they don't want people to tell them what to do. The more courageous people make their environment work for them, and that could mean changing your environment.

So what if you're staying? Finding intuitive and intentional practices to fill your everyday life will leave you that much more fulfilled. Opportunities will come your way, and you never know where the road will take you.

It's funny when you find out that there's a perception of you out there that people think you have covered all of your bases and you understand what you're doing. You have the reason why, and you're in alignment with your mission and your vision, and all that other shit that we spirituals say. Yet, in the meantime, I was still incredibly unsure of myself, and totally scared, but doing it anyway. I knew that I had no real choice - this was my path.

When you find out that people may have a different perception of you, good or bad, it proves that we're not always in control. There's even less of a reason to give a shit about what other people think of you, good or bad. Because at the end of the day, they're going to think something totally different than what you're anticipating anyway.

Even in my relief, and excitement, and nervousness about leaving, I was hearing the message loud and clear, that continuing to live my truth, and work through authenticity in those last few years made a huge impact - not just on me, but on my team. You might never know how much you're impacting someone (seemingly until you're gone).

Chapter 9
Finding the Right Seat

I was lucky enough to be in a viable enough position to leave my kush flexible corporate gig and explore the world of entrepreneurship. For me, this was in alignment, despite all the scary unknown future things. But, I'd been living in 3 worlds for 2 years when I left - I had an active side gig, opened a brick and mortar wellness center, and was working full-time. It was time to drop one, and it certainly wasn't going to be what felt to me like the rest of my life.

My story, along with other 'corporate turned entrepreneur' stories, is a bit dramatic. Just watch any episode of Shark Tank and you'll find a sobbing business owner telling the heroic story of giving it all up for their microfiber sham cloth (still waiting for your deal, Sharks). But... not all of us need this drama. Some of us are meant to be the leaders to stick around and make the world a better place for our teams, and ultimately, our organizations.

As we explored in Part 1, you first must know yourself, before you know others. Once you know you are at your soul level, you start to see the big picture and can start to align yourself within it. Alignment means finding the right seat for you on the bus of life and work.

Throughout my career, countless times I've identified inexperienced supervisors and managers placed in a position of power due to their superior knowledge or output of job tasks, but are left without the proper skills, knowledge, or learning techniques to manage people.

There are key differences between a task manager and a people manager. A task manager is well informed and skilled in both completing and managing the tasks required to successfully complete the assignments of any given position. This is generally the 'check the box' type activities that you'd find on a job description. A task manager's duties get into the nitty gritty of those tasks, including a good understanding of the how, the systems, the troubleshooting, and the standard of procedures (SoP) required to successfully complete those tasks in question. A people manager, on the other hand, is less concerned with the completion of the tasks themselves, and more concerned with the people that are currently in those positions completing those tasks. A people manager monitors overall performance, fit in the organization, growth of that employee, and of their team as a whole. They provide coaching more so than mentorship. A very skilled people manager will also understand a great deal about the tasks at hand, and perhaps has direct experience in completing and managing those tasks, but it is not always a requirement, given solid skillset in coaching.

Unfortunately, this is painting a very utopian picture of management. More often than not, an employee is great at their job, so they're asked to train others. Once they train others, they're placed in a position of team lead or authority over others. Team lead leads to supervisor, supervisor leads to manager, manager leads to director, and all these 'level-ups' come with a giant lack of training, support, or growth for that great employee who's now responsible for a large organization. They were never given the people management skills needed to help their team thrive. And *surprise*: they're burned out. In addition to never gaining appropriate people management skills, they also never learned to offload work, to seek support, to create boundaries, and to *breathe* on their way up the ladder. Just because you're great at your job, does not mean you're great at leading people. It's the cold hard truth fam.

. . .

Here's the kicker - you can even be great at leading people - but, also absolutely hate it. And what good is that doing you, or your team? You gotta get the right people on the right seats on the bus.

Here we go with the bus talk. Here's the deal. There's a bus that's arriving and taking all of us from where we are to where we want to go. There's a lot of people involved in operating this bus, and it's not dissimilar to running a company:

Bus Driver => People Managers

The bus driver knows where the bus is currently, they know where the bus has to go, and they know all the planned stops along the way. They're not necessarily responsible for who got on the bus and who gets off, but they can certainly influence and control the comings and goings of the passengers. If they miss a stop or stop too quickly and passengers don't move as they need to, they're sure to be blamed, but maybe the mechanics slipped up and an axle wasn't efficiently repaired, or the logistics manager didn't account for a new itinerary. Or, maybe, they just weren't given the route, didn't ask for it, and shouldn't be a bus driver and are better suited to be a passenger or mechanic.

· · ·

135

Passengers => Independent Contributors

There's no bus without passengers. Passengers are the only reason a bus exists, but the bus is there to provide a service to other passengers. Some passengers are on the bus for a while, others just are on and off, and they're not going anywhere without the bus driver. Some are completely fine riding along, while others strive to do more. Sometimes the passengers have a bad day, and it doesn't matter how great the driver is, the passenger just isn't happy.

Mechanics => Administrators

A lot of people don't see them, don't think about them, and certainly aren't concerned about them until something breaks. They can make or break a smooth bus ride, and be really expensive, but the bus doesn't get built or run without the mechanic. They can also provide a ton of preventative maintenance to proactively ensure breakdowns won't happen when they don't need to.

Logistics Manager => Task Managers

These guys don't just know the routes, they run and design the routes. They could tell each passenger exactly where each stop is, how long it will take to get there, and even plan out their next trip. They probably could even drive the bus in a pinch, but maybe they don't have full license to do so, and certainly aren't guaranteed to be the best at customer service. They need a little help from the bus drivers before they can become a full bus driver themselves. And again - maybe they are totally cool with being the logistics manager.

Ticket checker => Recruiters

"Hey, are you even supposed to be on this bus?!"

I think you get it. Employees are certainly capable of being more than a passenger, but some don't want to, and others can be given all the tools and resources possible, and still just not have the skillset of the logistics manager or the bus driver. Just because you're good at riding the bus, does not mean you can drive it, and most certainly not be responsible for other passengers.

The key is finding the right role for the right people. All of the people are necessary. But not all of the people can be given a checklist or a book, and suddenly be amazing in their new role. The guy that makes the pizza

137

dough hasn't always proven to be the best front end manager, but every once in a while you get lucky and the skills, the passion, and the knowledge all add up.

Every individual is responsible for their own growth, and responsible for seeking help from others when it's necessary. In order to identify your strengths and opportunities, you first need to fully understand oneself. As a conscious leader, you have to meet people where they're at, and figure out how to get yourself there first.

Through my own early adulthood, personal struggles, and constant overcoming of obstacles, it had become apparent that my strength was in educating others; specifically, in effectively managing leaders, teams, communication, and conflict resolution. I can attribute the very beginning of this journey to that day at Barnes and Noble, picking up that book from the self-help stack. Without understanding my current state, what resources I needed to grow, my own commitments to succeed, and my truth, I would never have been able to work my way from passenger to logistics manager to bus driver.

The 'a-ha' moments experienced by managers and colleagues as they develop these skills for themselves are the reason I love what I do. I strive to create these understandings through laughing, real-life experiences, and encouraging discussion and collaboration. The irony is that my biggest lesson in expansion came from being triggered into laughing at someone's struggle stated in a book title, and then realizing that same phrase was exactly the lesson I needed to learn; 'Will I Ever Be Good Enough?' Yes... yes I would. This began my journey into knowing myself, and recognizing the need for growth and intuitive connection in others.

Starting your journey of knowing yourself is as easy as starting to live an intentional life. This sounds fancy - it really just means waking up and reminding yourself of a purpose. Write your mission vision and values on a post-it on your desk. Make it fancy - frame it. Or go digital and make it your desktop background.

Remind yourself daily, weekly, monthly, as often as it takes. What seat do you want to sit in, and what seat are you in now? Check in with yourself on your seat on the bus on a quarterly basis. If you find you need a shift, you'll know it's time to put pen to paper to begin your next manifestation journey.

Chapter 10

I Get By With a Little Help from my Friends

The Mystery Woman

My intuition led me to some amazing opportunities in my career. After 3 years of absolutely killing it as a traveling HR Consultant, our team started hearing whispers about this brand new level of client service that was in the making. Word on the street was that our team would somehow be involved if it really got off the ground.

Now, at the time, things in my life were pretty much on auto-pilot. My daughter was in Kindergarten and didn't require a whole lot of Mommy time like before. My clients were super happy. I had a great sales partner who I really enjoyed spending my days with. My team was so good. My boss was great. Things were great... and boring. Out of the millions of things I could do to pick up the pace a bit, the last thing in the world I thought I'd do is consider going back to school (because

140

why would I just sit and enjoy the easiness...) Something told me, "Now is the time to go get your Masters." Again, this was something I *never* thought I'd do. I am not a great student in the formalized education system. I like making up my own rules. And until this point, I'd been pretty successful without it. Alas, I followed my gut.

I applied and was accepted to the online Graduate program for Adult Education at SUNY Buffalo State. My most favorite part of HR was learning and development and I had a knack for creating and rolling out programs and training, particularly in the work environment. So.. off I went.

About 3 seconds after my first semester started, we were called to a team meeting with our Director. Guess what. "You're going to be heavily involved in this new pilot and it's going to be a HUGE shift and change and take a lot more of your time..." Perfect. So that was it. Off into this new world with no rules and trials and spreadsheets and new partners and difficulty, all with my school laptop, books, and endless post-it notes in tow.

Turns out, I freaking loved my program (minus one class that was my nemesis). It was so much different than undergrad. You were surrounded by people that actually were interested in what they were learning. Most of us were full-time employees and the majority of us were in HR in some capacity.

With the new program taking off, and my interest in making sure my team was performing up to snuff, I reached out to my Director. I sent her an email saying something like I wasn't really sure how I fell into the strategy of this program, but I had a lot of observations (i.e. obsessions), was passionate about the impact to client service, and "I need to be in the driver's seat for this." That email opened up an ongoing dialogue about being proactively involved in this big project.

As I kept studying, I found a nice overlap with my program and the growing need for training within my team for navigating this pilot. I was able to use a lot of my real work as a basis for my studies. I worked closely with my leaders to gain a very thorough understanding of where this pilot program was headed and used proven adult education theories to facilitate learning at a level I could influence.

About a year went by, and I got a call from my boss. He said a new position was becoming available in our Corporate Learning & Development team to help facilitate the official rollout of the model across the Country. He told me he didn't think there was anyone better fit for this role than me. I had to say, I agreed.

. . .

Part of this new role - a huge change moving from front service lines in a division to a Corporate position - included working closely and like a first mate to both the Training Manager and another woman whom I had not met, knew little about, and wasn't really sure of the purview of her job due to the weirdness of the pilot. After a couple of conversations with the Training manager, I knew it was my gig. I still went through the entire (extremely formal and drawn out) interview process, but I just knew I had it in the bag. Plus I made her laugh a ton, and that's led me to lots of beneficial places in life.

This other woman, however, I had no idea how to get 'in' with her. She was not going to be my boss, we worked for entirely different divisions, and I knew very little about her personally (despite my recon efforts through internal and external sources). About 6 months before this new training job became available, I asked for an exploratory conversation to learn more about her team. The process was disjointed and never panned out. I felt a little sidelined. Like, what the heck, I've put in all this work, built relationships, put myself out there, and I can't even get a phone call? Cue the hair flip and the *whatevs*.

. . .

But, I got the Training job, and my first big mission for myself was to get to know this mystery woman. Again, I had no 'real' reason why this was important. I just knew it was. And no one else seemed to really see that or think about it, which was always really confusing to me. She *was* the pilot. So much so that she tells a story about talking about the pilot so much that her son thought she literally flew a plane for a living. The first time I met her in person, I was like, "Oh my god... she's funny, she's super smart, she's influential, she's gorgeous, and I need to be her go to person." *Fangirled* It was my own personal mission to meet her and know her at a real human level.

About a month into the new job, it was showtime. We were out of pilotville and into transformation town. One of our first stops was in Kansas City. After a few long days of our training session, another training partner and I were heading back from dinner to the hotel in our Uber. She reported to my new BFF Mystery Lady. She casually mentioned that the mystery lady and a bunch of other people from the local team were hanging out at a bar, but not anyone we already knew. As I closed the door to the Uber, I was like, "We're going."

I walked into this dark dingy bar (my favorite of the kind) and ended up having one of the best nights of my life. I gathered all of the guts I had to muster, I went straight up to Mystery Lady and after a shot (or two) I straight up asked why she never connected with me. Like, who the hell am I?! She has no idea who I am. I have not proven myself to her at all. But, I knew this was the way to handle this situation; Take the shots together and put it all out on the table. The most professional thing I could think of, obviously.

We had a super open and honest conversation, fell in love, and the rest is history. Well, you don't really know the rest, but it's really good. The next morning, I woke up with a massive headache and gratitude radiating off the hotel door hinges. I was so proud of myself! I recognized that this was a person I wanted to know. I waited for an opportunity to really show her my authentic self. I really went after a tough conversation and knew I made a great work partner. I did not anticipate making a wonderful friend.

The next day in the airport flying home, I perused the souvenir shelves. Knowing I would be doing a lot of travel in that year, I decided to take home 1 souvenir from each city I went to. I was going to grab another mug to add to my collection, but behind the mug was a little upside down yellow glass lightbulb. Printed on the outside of the bulb was the phrase "I got Lit in Kansas City." How appropriate. And what a great reminder of what happens when you really follow your gut. Consider it purchased.

• • •

To make a long story long, we spent the next year spending what felt like every waking moment together strategically, and comically rolling out our shared beloved model to over 700 HR professionals, impacting $40 Billion in business. Woah. After that year, we knew the model, the division, our partners, and our clients up, down, backwards, and forwards. With her support and partnership, I was able to create a new position for myself in strategy and support for the field. Another step up the rung of the ladder. More responsibility (more money!), new partners, and new projects. I rocked on that train for a bit which turned into my Coaching position reporting directly to her for the last 3 years of my life in Corporate. On top of all of the other amazing things about her, it turns out she is the best leader I've ever had the privilege of working with.

Not only is she still one of the funniest, smartest, influential, and gorgeous people I know, but she is a lifelong friend. And SOMEDAY, we want to start a podcast.

I tell you this story for a few reasons, and not just because it's fun and reveals what a sucker I am for jokes and dingy bars. It illustrates how important it is to follow your intuition, even without data in the corporate world. I had plenty of reasons why it would make sense to move forward with my Masters, explore a new job, and meet a mysterious lady, but none of them really needed to happen. I could have stayed in my other position forever. It was easy, convenient, flexible, I had a great leader and team, I was really good at it, I loved (almost) all my clients. I could have been happy enough there. I just knew something else was on the horizon. I had no idea what... but I needed to be in the driver's seat.

Secondly, it really shows the importance of partnership and a support system. Particularly in a corporate environment! Go back through and catalog the relationships I fostered just in this one story that led me from walking in the door as a Consultant and walking out the door as a Coach (and local work witch). It was through my intuition and influencing skills that I was able to form a crucial partnership and friendship that would guide me through the happiest and toughest times in the corporate rat race.

How to be Irreplaceable in Corporate

It wasn't until after I'd reached the top of my own corporate ladder, climbing rung by rung, that I recognized I did something pretty special, and also pretty intuitively. I never thought much about the steps I had to take... I just did them. It was like someone was guiding me the entire way, without a logical linear process to follow. I started getting phone calls from other consultants asking for advice on how I navigated my career, as they were looking to duplicate the same path. Sometimes I had no idea what to tell them!

I'd talk about the importance of trial and error and partnerships. Put yourself out there; jump on projects that seemingly don't matter; call people up to ask about their day-to-day and ask how you can support them. These are all seemingly high-level pieces of advice, and they are valuable. But I was doing something just a bit more. I decided to create a process that anyone could follow or understand, using both structured advice, and incorporating each individual's intuition.

We ran through the clairs back in chapter 2. Each person, regardless of spirituality, has clairs and likely multiples of them. The question isn't 'Which ones do I have', it is 'Which comes most easily and which do I have to develop?' Each person is on their own spiritual development path, and has differing levels of understanding of their intuitive gifts. For this reason, using intuition to create consciousness in the corporate world is not a straightforward 1, 2, 3, step situation. My mission was to make it as clear as possible, with room to work with you where you're at in your intuitive development. BEHOLD! The key to becoming irreplaceable at work, all while using your intuition.

OBSERVE

Watch what's going on around you.

Starting with your energy body:

- What and who are you drawn towards? Where do you feel that draw?
- Is it in your chest? (This is a heart connection - this is clairsentience)
- In your gut? (This is a solar plexus connection - this is also clairsentience)
- Can you see where things are developing and need to be a part of it? (This is a third eye connection - this is clairvoyance)

Tapping into your environment:

- Who's working together well?
- Who works well with no one?
- Who's gossiping?
- Who's keeping things close to the vest?
- Who is seemingly successful in your eyes? Who is not?
- Who is leading meetings, what is their title, and main job responsibilities?
- Who do they talk to?

Be aware of the actual organizational chart, and the informal organizational chart.

• • •

I Get By With a Little Help from my Friends

Informal organization is determined by cross-department relationships, interactions, and project members. Know who reports to who, and who actually gets things done with who.

- Who holds influence and power?
- What is their story and how did they get there?
- Who did they partner with?

LISTEN

This used to be easier when we were "in office". If you're onsite and sitting at a desk, pay attention to the conversations people are having. Don't go tapping any phones or anything, but listen to the topics of discussion. Pay attention to the emotional response and the task related response.

Starting with your energy body:

Block your calendar, go on Do Not Disturb, close your door, and put in your noise canceling headphones

Sit in silence, or have some pineal gland music playing (minimum 5 minutes)

. . .

As you enter into silent mode, ask yourself:

- What do I hear?
- What do I need to be paying attention to?
- Who in my work life can give me opportunities?
- Who in my work life can help with my development?

In your environment:

- Who's working on what?
- What's interesting, what's gossip, and what could you assume might be possibilities based on those calls?
- Does it sound like a cool possibility? Is it something you could get involved with?
- If not, what could you do that is in line with that same initiative?

Chances are if you're working parallel, you'll be brought into the project with a different perspective than those already involved. And if you're not asked, you can present the ideas and the work you've already done on your own and it will fit right in. Don't be afraid to do work that's not part of your expectations (if it's something that actually interests you).

Caution: Be aware of going way outside the realm of your responsibilities if it's not something that you can also prove ties back to your own work. Get buy-in from your immediate leader and make them aware of all big projects you take on. You never know what will take off, and who you'll need at your back to showcase your work and support your efforts.

UNDERSTAND

When you've already taken care to observe and listen, you'll start to develop your own understanding of the situation. However, you have filters. And your filters are most definitely in play to develop that 'reality'. It's important to never stop asking questions, even when you think you have the answers.

In your energy body:

- How does the information make you feel, and where do you feel it?
- Can you see how this situation might play out? What are some options?

. . .

In your physical environment:

Through observing and listening, you'll have learned the who's who and the what's what. Now when you ask questions, you'll have the context around the answer you receive. You'll also be able to frame your question to others from the more intelligent lens of already knowing some basic information that you collected through your initial 'research' of observing and listening.

Don't take the first answer for granted. Keep in mind the answers you're getting, and from who you're getting them from. They have filters too, and their understanding could also not be totally accurate. Based on your initial observations, you'll probably find that you already have a pretty accurate idea of the type of answer you'll get.

When you already have an answer, ask the question again to someone else. Then ask again of someone else. See how you receive that information - is it the same or different? Compare and contrast the answers.

You'll learn who knows how much of what topics, who is working with who, and who has the most influence in that topic. You'll learn more about the subject itself, and also figure out who you can trust and who you should avoid.

Caution: Don't "answer shop". I've come across lots of colleagues who make their mind up about their reality - without observing or listening. Now they're shopping around and asking questions, only looking for an answer that lines up with their assumptions, and looking for an agreement or permission to do what they want to do in the first place. This is not the same as fully understanding all the players and facts before coming to a holistic understanding of a situation. This is a lot like the "mom/dad" game we're familiar with as a kid. "Dad, can I go to the movies?" "No." "But Mom said I could...." Ew. You're not 12 anymore.

CONNECT

Make it happen!

After you've done all the groundwork, you'll have a good idea about who's the best to partner with on which projects or initiatives. You'll learn what's on the horizon and what possibilities there are for you. At this point you'll have enough information and previously established relationships via your conversations to be able to provide context for new people you want to bring in, and start conversations with others who are already involved.

Any choice you make at this point is educated. Even if you started with your intuition, you've backed it up with facts.

Maybe the most important part about 'connection' is being authentic.   What if you did all this work, approached a great partner, started to build something together, then they found out you're not at all who you painted yourself to be? You've given yourself the chance to observe and listen independently - you might as well make sure that what you decide to understand and connect with is something that's truly aligned with the real you!

We can't always know the best way to go, or the clearest path to take, but you can certainly control what you did to arrive there. Safe travels!

Interview with an Intuitive Leader

The year was 2017. I was a Graduate Student at SUNY Buffalo State studying Adult Education. One of four million papers was on my to-do list, and this one required an interview from a corporate professional on their career development. I talked to a guy named

Mike. He was a Software Engineering Support Manager nearing the end of his thirty-six-year career at the large tech firm. What I wrote then felt important. As I conducted the interview, I knew this story was unique and somehow played into something bigger in my life. I'd like to share that essay with you now:

Let It Roll: Using Intuition to Guide a Career

In 1981, Mike started a career that would lead him from technician to upper management of a giant tech corporation. After starting his career as a technician, he made simultaneous career and life decisions guided by doing what felt right given his personal and educational standings at the time. He holds the belief that these decisions guided his success by building his own knowledge, respecting his teams, and serving his customers; internal, external, and personal.

Without realizing his drive, Mike discussed his career's actions and decisions with me which I came to find as an undoubtedly intuitively led career.

In his youth, Mike had an ongoing and increasing interest in electronics. His older brother worked as a technician in the Navy and his Grandfather dabbled in the electronic world, especially in building his own radios. He was exposed to this work early on and somewhat mentored by his family which reinforced and supported these interests. In his late teens, Mike strived to be a technician, particularly in a lab environment or out in the field servicing equipment. He considered multiple higher education opportunities, in addition to the Navy. He turned down the Navy and a school in Chicago for Penn State, which offered a two-year associate degree in Electronics Engineering at the Altoona, Pennsylvania campus.

While studying at Penn State, Mike had a professor who came from Rochester who purchased five of the first desktop computers. In the late 1970s, this type of desktop computer was unheard of; they were only owned by schools. Working with these computers was what allowed Mike to write his first software program. His end-of-the-year project was to create any program of the students' choice. He chose to write a horse racing program that included random number generators. He still enjoys the race track today – I know this because Mike is my father. His most recent bet was on a horse named Kissin Cassie; a sure bet in his mind, because my daughter's name is Cassie.

Mike tends to make decisions based on intuition. This was my word for what he described as, "just knowing" and "it just made sense." When asked how he has remained at one company for thirty-six years, despite numerous financial setbacks, downsizing, leadership changes, and global outsourcing, his answer was because he was surrounded by people he started the job with. They all 'climbed the corporate ladder'. He never had any intention of becoming anything more than an individual contributor, but he was forced to make a life-changing decision in 1985.

Mike started his career as a Test Technician, testing the software used during the lifecycle of copiers. Less than a year into that position, he took a position as a technician supporting the software lab. He was fortunate enough to have a mentor that saw his interest and talent in developing code as it existed then. The mentor and managers would present him with a code which he had to fix. He began writing proprietary software – the first existing multi-tasking language. Mike wanted to continue down his career development path in software engineering, so he started a four-year program at Rochester Institute of Technology in Software Engineering.

In 1985, Mike was presented with a choice in his career that could have changed his entire life. He had the opportunity to stay where he was at and continue his degree, or join the "Tiger Team" who traveled the world serving customers. At this same point in his life, he had met a young woman with three young children and entered a serious relationship. He had just built his first home, and his love interest was just about to move in. The thought of not finishing his degree was scary, but the thought of dealing with his girlfriend's response was scarier. His girlfriend is now my Mother; I can attest to this terrifying feat.

Mike weighed this option considering all of the external factors. Does it make sense to continue his degree for long-term success? Does he stick around for his girlfriend? Does he go and travel the world?? An impossible decision for someone who doesn't truly know who they are. Mike made an intuitive decision and supported his reasoning based on his value set. For someone else, it could have been a different decision. And such is the beauty of life! The same circumstances could lead to different paths.

Erik Erikson's theory of early adulthood includes a note of learning decisions often being centered around intimacy. In the text "Learning in Adulthood", S.B. Merriam states, "In young adulthood, the successful resolution between intimacy versus isolation results in love." Science and theory meet heart - my kinda topic.

Mike decided to continue with his school program and continue as a lab technician, ultimately doing what's natural to him; making a decision that "just made sense." He married in 1986, and, "had this baby in '88 that really threw [him] for a loop!" (Thanks, Lindsay.)

In addition to his personal situation, the decision made sense for his career. He knew the hardware and software inside and out since he'd been working on it since its invention. The copiers he built were now a ten-billion-dollar business; the traditional market was flat and going digital. The company needed experts who could move into the digital world, and he'd become an expert. It was a natural choice that he continued to work on for fifteen years, until he was asked to manage a group of 12 engineers.

I asked Mike what made him a successful manager. After first saying it was 'canceling meetings because they're just a big bitch session' (so true), he said "Everybody tells me that people want to work for me because I respect them and what they do." I responded, "Is that because you did it?" "Yes! That's a big part. I know what they do, and what they go through."

Unfortunately the company had not been successful in recent years. Mike attributes the difficulties to a change in leadership and taking the company away from its roots. Unsuccessful acquisitions were funded by an otherwise successful service division. He also discussed social changes. "We don't do things like we used to. Big launch parties, team lunches, they don't emphasize these achievements any longer." He organizes small events for his team, but nothing happens at an upper management level any longer. He also lacks the same relationships he used to with middle and upper management. "I knew everyone because we worked together. They're all gone. I don't know the voices around the table on the conference calls anymore. A lot of them I haven't even seen before." Victims of layoffs, downsizing, outsourcing, most of his peers have left in the last ten years. If they weren't told to leave, they chose to in order to avoid that fate. Last week, Mike received his second voluntary reduction in force package. He has chosen to pass on it this time around, but suspects that he will receive an involuntary package in the spring, and if he does not, he will be voluntarily retiring.

Mike worked on the first computers, copiers, and printers, and holds three patents for his work. He was there at the beginning of computer technology and has seen it advance. Unfortunately, a successful thirty-six-year career has resulted in a pending retirement to hopefully avoid a layoff. Mike has been what he calls 'lucky' to avoid so many previous layoffs, but I call it consciously leading. If he had not led a team and allowed them to successfully do their jobs, without getting in their way, he may have been asked to leave a long time ago. Throughout the interview, he emphasized his appreciation of personal relationships built through teams, and then continuing as a manager.

"My team is much better at the work than I am. I've been away from the intricacies of it for a long time. And the software's different, the functionality of the machines is different, it's areas I've never dealt with. I let them do their thing, and I just manage their problem sets – what's a priority, what's not. I manage what needs to be done, but don't tell them how to do it or what to do."

The money, work ethic, and personal relationships kept him in the business. "My personal life drove the work ethic more than the company formed my personal life... My career has meant zilch to my personal life." Mike's advice to people early in the career: "You have to have pride in what you do and you're going to be successful. I've always felt that the money would follow. I never went in and begged for a raise or promotion – they always seemed to come. I never tried to climb the corporate ladder. I let it roll." Managing people and developing good relationships made it all worth his time, rather than, "climbing the corporate ladder and driving yourself crazy."

With wisdom, comes the advice: "You can't start a career thinking corporate is where the money's at. I think there's people that lack some of the values, but I wouldn't call it generational. I know a lot of younger people that are top notch. I don't buy into the 'younger generation isn't any good'. Every generation goes through that. Older generations think their way is the best way. That's bullshit, times change. There's a drive that exists with younger workers that doesn't exist with older workers. Better ideas come with more drive."

As someone ending his career, he, "never did any preparation. People probably should!" For ten years, he had the intention of figuring out what he wanted to do when the company no longer supported him. He's staring retirement in his face and has no idea what he'll do next.

"You'll want to think about it. The younger generation now knows what it's like to move between jobs. When you're in the middle you better figure out what you want to do next." He also added that all employees should find a way to shadow the front lines. "What's changed between then and now is that I'm more immediate at trying to find solutions. A deadline to a customer means more than what it did meeting corporate deadlines. You need to see that in your career. That's where the money's coming from. It's where your paycheck comes from. There are too many people far away from that kind of business."

. . .

The front lines: My dad has always been an advocate for serving the customer, whether that was for a work customer, his team, his parents, or his family.   If someone needs help, he's the first person to provide it. Not necessarily without its sarcastic comment, or gripe, but he's always a support. I've always looked to him as an expert in anything he puts his mind to, including his career. Turns out he's also an expert in following his intuition. I see my dad as an expert at doing life. Just like him, when given obstacles and forks in the road, I make intuitive decisions. I will forever hear his voice encouraging me to 'let it roll.'

As you read through my Dad's career story, you're able to see where he took some of the same intuitive steps I did, a lifetime later in my career. What's fascinating about this is that I was completely unaware of this at the time I'd already started developing my own intuitive skills. It goes to show you that we all have the capability to make decisions based on our intuition, even while we're at work.

Let's Get Practical

Read back through this story. Where do you see examples of Observe, Listen, Understand, Connect?

What would you have done?

Chapter 11
Workplace Energetics

What's the number one mistake I see new leaders make? Not having a plan. That's it. And I'm not talking about a 30-60-90 day plan or the big 35-page business plan document that everyone hates. I'm talking about a full leadership strategy that's rooted with a Mission, Vision, and Values, and allows room for creativity, expansion, flow, and a last minute "I JUST GOTTA DO THIS". Remember that practical exercise from Chapter 2? We'll use that same format to create your energetic plan for career development.

Entrepreneurial Spirit

When you stop thinking about your job as a requirement, and start thinking about it as an opportunity to build something of your own, you can make a huge mindset shift. You do NOT have to play by everyone else's rules. You may not be headed for hanging a shingle and opening your own business, but you are a leader. You can lead! You can lead how you see fit. I'm going to teach you how to bring the entrepreneurial spirit into your corporate life by working with... here they are again!... the Chakras.

Like we talked about before, each organization has its own energetic blueprint. Your team is no different. So when you're looking to infuse some energetic goodness into your everyday work, you can evaluate where you stand and where you want to go in growth from the lens of the Chakra system.

CROWN — INTUITIVE INFUSION — AWARENESS, INTELLIGENCE

THIRD EYE — FUTURE GOALS — INTUITION, IMAGINATION

THROAT — PERFORMANCE MANAGEMENT — COMMUNICATION & EXPRESSION

HEART — CONNECTIONS — LOVE, HEALING, COMMUNITY

SOLAR PLEXUS — TEAM CELEBRATIONS — JOY, LAUGHTER, CONFIDENCE

SACRAL — TEAM DEVELOPMENT — PLEASURE, CREATIVITY

ROOT — FINANCIAL — STABILITY, IDENTITY, GROUNDING

Starting with the Root, it represents stability, grounding, and identity. In business this means we ground with mission, vision, and values. I work with leaders first to identify a solid set of values aligned with oneself, then a set of values for their team that will not change as their team changes and grows. The mission and vision statements will allow the decision maker to consider ideas, or new launches, while staying in alignment with the organization and themselves. Questions to ask when making these decisions:

- Hiring a new employee or taking on a new partner? Do they share the same values?
- Do I need new systems? Do they support these values?
- Are we rolling out a new product or service offering? Does it fall in line with these values?
- Do we have a new customer or client? Do they subscribe to these values?

I know what you're thinking - I've been in your shoes. "Linds, there's just so much out of our control - sometimes I'm told to do something that's totally not in my value set and I just have to deal with it." If it's truly not in a value alignment, maybe you need to think bigger; Do I suck it up and still be miserable? Do I leave? Or do I stay and make lemonade out of some lemons?

The *VAST* majority of the time, squeeze them lemons baby. Maybe you're not in total alignment with what you're being required to do. But consider what you *do* have control of within your team and within yourself, to best utilize the skills, talents, and values that go along with this initiative. I would say it's only going to be in real extreme cases of ongoing misalignment (and likely ethical boundaries) that you should consider bouncing, rather than making some lemonade.

Moving onto the sacral, this is the pleasure and creativity center of the energetic body. This is where we'll define the type of conversations and topics you'll want to bring to your team. What will be individual workshops, and what will be ongoing lessons? When you tell other people about accomplishments as a leader, what will you want to showcase? What's in your team's secret sauce?

The solar plexus is your joy center. Here's the fun part where you get to create happiness on your team. How are you celebrating the work? Maybe you're not a huge fan of the output, but there's lots of people putting in lots of work to make it happen. Celebrate the dedication and the skillset, and the humans you have working with you. When you're working from joy and from creation, don't allow any of the "I shouldn'ts" or "I can'ts" exist here. "Why not?" is often my favorite question.

Next is the heart chakra. This represents the community and network you build with your team, your colleagues, your leaders, your division, and even customer or vendor channels.

The throat is your communication and expression. A natural area to determine your learning and development and performance management strategies. What's your most loved way to communicate? Make sure you're making this as easy on yourself as possible. Why go against your own energetic grain when you're the content creator? Be mindful of the 'corporate' rules, but meet your requirements, then make up the rest. As long as you've built up some level of responsibility and respect in your org, sometimes asking for forgiveness is better than asking for permission *heavy wink*.

Moving up, your third eye is your intuition and imagination. We'll look into the future a little bit here as we determine each aligned growth strategy. Along with a quarterly plan for the next year, some questions to ask yourself to determine how the next year should look: A year from now, what do you want your job to look like? What do you want your team to look like? A year from now, what do you want to be doing in your career that's different from today? How many hours a week are you working on average? What are your annual home/personal income goals? What are your annual income goals?

Lastly, we have the crown chakra. This is where you're encouraged to access your higher self, greater consciousness, and source. This is your break from work – your breather, your battery supply for the next big thing. Use all of your healing strategies from HEAL for this part of your growth strategy.

Let's Get Practical

Consult the cards:

- Pull an oracle card or tarot card for guidance on short term goals
- Schedule a reading with a pro; Shameless plug (www.lindsaymastro.com)
- Read for yourself using tarot spreads specific to each cycle
- Visit www.lindsaymastro.com/bookresources for an Intuitive Tarot Workbook with Leadership Spreads

Pretty up your aura and area with crystals:

- Keep a tigers eye and clear quartz crystal around you to aid in clarity and grounding for this new moon phase.
- Tigers eye brings excellent energy for providing courage, strength, confidence, and is associated with your root chakra. As you begin your journey towards intentional development, you'll want to remain grounded, start with the basics, and be clear in your intention moving forward.
- Clear quartz is the master healing crystal, is specifically used to bring about clarity, and can be used with any other energy as an amplifier.
- Create a crystal grid in your office.

Cleanse your physical space at work or at home

- Smoke cleanse with your herb of choice
- Sound cleanse with a bell, chime, or solfeggio frequencies
- Use an enchanted or intentional body & linen spray
- Light a white candle for clarity and a black candle for protection

Goal Setting

. . .

Set a business goal for the current lunar cycle, for the next quarter, and for the next year. Plan the information you'll need to truly achieve that goal.

Some examples of things to think about:

- How many new customers/clients would you like to service (this could be internal or external customers)
- How many new projects are you able to take on?

- Is your team operating efficiently? Do you need more or less headcount?
- Where can tasks be redistributed?
- Cross train your current team

- How many repeat customers/clients would you like to serve?

- Which skills would you like your individual direct reports to demonstrate?

- What are your revenue and profit targets?
- What would you like your customers/clients to achieve? How will you help them meet those goals?

- What new project will help align you with your mission and vision for your team?
- What will you need to meet those goals?

- What content/advertising/product/service will you
- need to offer to meet those goals?
- When and where will you advertise these products?

- Perform a Start, Stop, Continue exercise
- What do you want to start? (Address new goals)
- What do you want to stop? (What can you clear out that no longer is working or needed?)
- What's working and what should you keep doing?

- What support do you need? (Who and what)

Chapter 12
Striving for Authenticity

I had lunch with a friend who was talking about her 'working her magic' as a leadership consultant. Unlike my path, she kept her magic under wraps, but still showed up authentically each day to lead other leaders. When she asked how I'd incorporated my gifts into work, and been not-so-quiet about it, she was encouraged that she could start tapping into her intuitive gifts, knowingly, rather than running in the background. She said something that echoes in my brain constantly. She said she could start doing this more loudly, but "do they really need to know I'm a wizard?" I never stop laughing about this. NO! They definitely don't need to know you're a wizard. But... a wizard should never leave home without his wand up his sleeve.

So bring your wand! It's up to you if you wanna go all 'Expecto patronum' about it.

Four Lies and a Truth

Authenticity is the driver for all things I do in life and in business. Remember when you were a kid and you played make-believe? Maybe you played 'house', or 'school'. Or, like me, if you were destined for the biz life, you played 'video store' and pretended to rent out all of your Disney VHS tapes from your very own basement Blockbuster.

At some point we stopped playing make-believe. Life gets a little more complicated than basement Blockbuster and we have real dreams, desires, and goals that we pour our energy into. The path to achieve those goals may look something like this:

- Step 1: Get good grades, so you can get into a good college.
- Step 2: Study hard in college so you can land an internship.
- Step 3: Be a great intern and land your first big girl (or boy) job.
- Step 4: Live happily ever after.

The thing is... we spend all that time, effort, and hard work to get to somewhere we think we want to be. But how much did you ever stop that game of make-believe, really? You hit your 20s, you're thrown into the business world, and suddenly you're still that kid playing make-believe, but this time you're wearing a suit. What happened to that kid? What happened to you...the real you?

Let's look at some of the lies we tell ourselves that keep us from professional authenticity.

Lie #1: I don't act 'like a professional.'

Certainly you can't be this business professional and aspiring executive and embrace all that you did as a growing person. How could you possibly be into Blink 182, and also be an expert at recruiting? Your amp broke a long time ago and you're too dizzy to keep riding that skateboard. Likely, you adapt. You become some version of who you think you should be to fit into this new weird world you've built for yourself.

The secret to becoming one whole person at work is to embrace your full selves and foster your innate gifts at work, so you can truly practice professional authenticity.

. . .

Professional authenticity - what does that even mean? Professional authenticity is bringing your innate gifts to the surface to communicate and execute your vision in a professional setting.

You know my story. I lost my way for quite a while. I faked some version of who I was and avoided my reality for a very long time. I knew I had a gift of seeing spirit, but I was never really driven to explore or develop that gift. Mostly because without appropriate teaching and knowledge, I was afraid of it. That 'stuff' didn't really fit into my idea of what a 'real life' should look like. Spirits and a 'real' job? No way.

I found another passion in my young adulthood in the big, deep, and mysterious world of Human Resources. Bit of a difference from the spirit world, no? Nevertheless, it was a passion of mine - the perfect combination of business operations and sociology. I also was just really good at it. But I find that's the case with passion; if you are passionate, you are invested, you are dedicated, you have the want to learn and experience more. In that, inevitably, you will rock your shit.

Lie #2: Success equals happiness.

. . .

I'm one of the lucky ones who found a way to foster my passion at work. This didn't mean that I was completely and fully satisfied in every position and in every company I worked for; quite the opposite. This just meant that no matter what I was doing, I would find what drove me. What made me want to move in a forward direction. But if passion was the secret, then why wasn't I happy?

Answer: Somewhere along the way, my authenticity dropped off the charts. I was good at what I did for a myriad of reasons, but my overwhelmingly consistent feedback was that people loved working with me because I was "genuine" and "casual" and "familial." I constantly struggled with this otherwise very positive message because... was I? I showed up to work every day completely and totally hiding the fact that even as you might be standing in my office, I might be receiving messages unheard and unseen. Because that's not what you're supposed to do, right? That's weird. It's personal. And then if you knew that, maybe you wouldn't like me... God forbid.

Lie #3: They won't like the real me.

Instead, I ignored those very loud and overwhelming messages, shoved them out of the way to focus on just the employee in my office, and would offer guidance and advice that somehow always helped the employee find their own way. All the while...I constantly seemed to be getting in my own way and becoming frustrated that something felt like it was missing. The coach often can't coach themselves.

I was fortunate enough in my career journey to find a company that values individuals and their innate gifts, and sees the value in educating employees. My personal values synced with the vision of the company. I had a supported and shared belief that when you provide a supportive environment for employees and leaders, company success will follow.

After years of soul searching, self-improvement, and straight up being tired of faking it, I was ready to start my new, truly authentic life. I'm striving to help you find a practical way to infuse intuition into your work. But this does not happen overnight folks.

Lie #4: That's not what executives do.

The reactions I have received after sharing my truth of being a medium on a large scale, and becoming more confident in expressing this with new acquaintances, has been nothing less than positive, supportive, and just overall lovely. I was terrified to share this, and once I did, I immediately felt I could embrace that label of 'genuine', 'authentic', and 'real', instead of just sorta kinda half-way there.

I also had the misconception that revealing my full self meant I had to change. I was pretty happy about my work, and how I presented myself professionally. But that authenticity piece couldn't really truly come forward until I was not only honest with others, but ultimately with myself.

The Truth: We are all just people.

Those thought leaders or business executives you follow and admire... they're people, just like you and me. They all go home and have to call their parents. They get annoyed when someone else finishes the ice cream in the freezer. They stub their toes on furniture in their house. They used to play make-believe...maybe they still do.

And if you find yourself in the position as a thought leader or executive, don't forget to fix the amp, throw on that old Blink182 album, dream up your next tattoo, read your emails, create your PowerPoint presentations, and run through your speaker's notes. Maybe think twice about busting out the old skateboard, though.

Bottom line: there's no one way to live your life, but however you choose to live it, keep it real.

Can I Get Some Feedback?

"We want you to be authentic." That's what all the bigwigs say. Do they really though? Words like 'authentic' 'creative' and 'innovative' are thrown around a lot in values statements and cultural pillars, but when you show up as your authentic creative and suggestive self and boots hit the proverbial pavement, you might find some confusing 'feedback' from leaders.

Let's talk about feedback in the workplace. Any leader will come to the point in their job where they'll have to deliver some feedback to their team. Good feedback is always great news. It's when something isn't quite jiving and not too great feedback has to be provided that gives everyone pause. And, I mean, everyone. Unless you are an actual sociopath who's energy gears up when tearing others down... then you don't like giving 'bad news'. This isn't for you - this is for the normies, the learning, the learned, and the conscious leaders out there.

. . .

I'm on a mission to bring some optimism to the word feedback in the work setting.

As a leader, you've observed or received news of some undesirable performance or behaviors from someone on your team. As you craft your delivery (not for the faint of heart), ask yourself the following questions:

- Is this information helpful right now?
- Is this information helpful for later?
- Does my version of later match this person's idea of later?
- Is this information necessary to appropriately achieve success in this role or the next?
- Does my version of success match this person's idea of success?
- Have I had a conversation with this person to understand their goals and passions?
- Am I the right person to deliver this feedback?
- Have I critically evaluated the situation that created this feedback to ensure it's based in truth?
- Am I prepared to handle a challenged reaction?

That last question is important. Don't be so quick to put some feedback out there, unless you're willing to get some in return. You also should prepare yourself to do something with return feedback coming your way. It's the number one failure I see in employee engagement programs. Endless surveys and suggestion boxes that are either never read, or the anticipated change is made without regard for the feedback received.

Now you're putting both your authenticity and integrity at risk if you're putting some feedback out there without considering how it might be received. If you have a business solution based on data, and don't intend on swaying from that, then don't offer a chance to rebut with options. It will leave a bad taste in your team's mouths when they're ignored without an opportunity to continue to follow up. You can be assertive when needed, hold space for an emotional reaction, and also explain when there's no fork in the road.

A Not-So Calculated Misstep

About 6 weeks after I left corporate, I was on the struggle bus trying to figure out why all of my well documented strategic efforts were going nowhere. I was annoyed that all the things you're "supposed to do" weren't panning out... including paid services and a sales partner. I'd aligned my HR consulting with the newly emerging New York State Cannabis industry - a sure thing.

. . .

But was it? A brand new industry doesn't happen a ton. It's not just the permitted sale of the product itself, it's all of the ancillary products and business support that come with it! SO much opportunity here, so much progress and creativity to be explored! This is totally my wheelhouse. When states are dictating the sale and consumption of an item, there's bound to be some leaders and laggers in the market. I was excited to jump in on this brand new opportunity. Surely, leaders needed development, and executives needed strategy and regulatory support. However, my big green world came crashing down after a progression of a few trade shows, political meetings, and partnering with developing industry groups. It had become abundantly clear... the state was not going to make this easy on employers.

I was a bit naive in my alignment with the industry as well. I look at everything from an employer and business perspective. I had *my* filters up too high - I was thinking too far ahead of where these businesses were at. I failed to recognize that you can't even worry about being an employer, if you're not legally allowed to get your business off the ground.

And while all this is happening, enter, the HR strategist preaching about ROI on employee experience. All true, all beneficial, but People Strategy ROI goes out the window when their business is at risk by merely operating. I can yell the percentage impact on retention, turnover and employee claims all day, but who's listening?

Therein lies the problem with New York Cannabis. How are you supposed to work with business leaders on strategy and organizational development, if there's no organization to be had?

I obviously had made a mistake - when making my plan for growth, I only checked in with what "made sense" on paper. And I was eager to get my HR business up and running 'legitimately" after just saying PEACE OUT to corporate life. I skipped my entire energetic process. I never checked in with my energy body, I didn't work through my manifestation cycle, I stopped paying attention to my moons. Like WHAT had happened to me, in such a short period of time? How could I fall so far out of my authentic alignment?

When I left corporate, knowing I'd be dabbling in HR and energy work, I decided to split my work weeks. I restructured my week; Monday - Wednesday were for Business. Thursday - Saturday were for Spirit. I really struggled with this because it inherently went against all my coaching for the past 3 years. I'd been out there preaching that you can do both! I went against my own coaching, and when I did, I left all the intuition out of the business piece.

. . .

I felt like I had to focus focus focus on getting things off the ground. The NYS Cannabis environment didn't make for a very great foundation for take off, despite its promising outlook. But, at the end of the day, it wasn't the external environment that made me take pause and re-evaluate. It was the fact that what I was truly passionate about and aligned with... WAS working, and WAS beneficial. I had discounted energy work because I still wasn't fully considering it "legitimate".

So after that brief soiree into being a weed people expert (still leaving room for that by the way...), I tapped back into my intuition and things have fallen in line. Sometimes the universe picks you up and sets you down where you're supposed to be when you refuse to take the wheel and hit the gas.

Imposter Syndroming

Out on my own for the first time, I fell victim to the "I'm not good enough" trap. I lost my 'mojo' and started questioning absolutely every decision I made. YIKES. Totally not a Lindsay thing, and I wasn't myself. Now looking back, I was totally out of touch with my intuition. Still not feeling capable of my own energetic pick-me-up, I scheduled a Reiki session with an incredibly powerful healer and friend of mine. Reiki is a Japanese energy healing modality that allows the practitioner to use universal energy (ki) to heal your energy and physical bodies. When in doubt, turn to energy work. Our conversation during the session was just what I needed.

She picked up that I was depleted. It wasn't that I wasn't trying - I was putting a ton of energy out there. But I wasn't charging myself up appropriately. She said, "Of course you're tired! You had to scrape the bottom of the barrel for no answer." That's what it was... I had a barrel in front of me that was the opportunity to dive into a new industry. I knew there was something in it because all the facts on paper said 'there should have been.' But, I dug and dug and dug, and there was nothing left in there. At least not right now.

I was more than a little clogged up in my chakras. I felt guilty because I kept changing things in my business. I was giving myself the false impression that "consistency is key" and that's the way it has to be. I said, "Ughhhh, I just feel bad about making so many changes all the time. I need to be more consistent." she said, "Why do you feel that way... do whatever you want! Why can't you keep changing things?"

My loud guttural and stubborn response was, "CUZ!" Many people might cry or get emotional during an energy session, but we laughed for about 15 minutes. Pretty on brand.

. . .

She was totally right. And it was the same advice I'd give to a client. We get in our own way.

Who heals the healer? Who fixes the plumber's leaky toilet? We all need another one of us to keep us on track. And the next best thing to another one of us is our own intuition - if you can manage to get your brain out of the way. My lovely Reiki lady is also an engineer. She's my kind of energy healer - one with a corporate base understanding and background, who also can rock the shit out of your chakras.

Riding the Line of Magic and Professionalism

I talk a whole lot about being conscious in corporate, but give me just a little bit to talk about the problem with being all conscious and NO corporate. As the news of my mediumship started to spread, I was approached by a lot of cool people for awesome opportunities. I've also been approached with some entirely weird and strange requests.

In one day, I got 2 voicemails from two different people I don't know, and have never heard of, within 20 mins of each other. The first person didn't even leave a name on their voicemail. They were inviting me to a "traveling psychic show." The second voicemail left slightly more info and name dropped a few people, so at least I could tell that it wasn't a joke.

Now, when you're a publicly practicing medium, gallery readings are just part of the gig. You can love it or hate it, choose to do it or not, but it's not weird to be asked about it. My issue with the whole request was... this is a business. No wonder energy work gets a bad rap. You've got people out here running the show who have no idea how to organize an event, much less advertise it in a way that will bring some level of mainstream recognition and appreciation for the work.

Would you rather go to a "traveling psychic show" or an "evening with spirit". Are we headed to a circus, or a supportive grieving space? Mediumship is not a sideshow. Energy work WORKS. But we need to do it some justice and start talking about it in a way that is inclusive to the rest of the world that isn't all that aware of it yet. You have to ride the line of healing, entertainment, and professionalism. You have to show up to the boardroom with all your magic, but without your witch hat. I found this wonderful balance of all three in corporate, and I hope that's what you're able to take from the stories and activities in this book. It's the only way to move forward and make some real change in our chaotic money-driven environments.

Change Management

"Change isn't easy." Isn't it? Change happens all the time, every minute of every day. I think the more appropriate phrase would be "The unknown is daunting." It's not the change itself that seems difficult, it's the 'what comes after' that's unsettling.

Managing change really just comes down to communication and empathy in its simplest form. At work, leaders stumble when trying to be 'too nice' rather than just openly communicate the steps that were taken in considering making a change.

If you are putting careful thought into making a change, then chances are you're already working at an empathetic level. It's the communication of this process that will typically result in hurt feelings and a feeling of being unheard/unseen by those that are affected by the change.

If you're in a corporation - you're going to deal with change. Sometimes things happen too fast, and sometimes too slow. It's important to remember that you can only control what you can on your impact level. You might not be able to pull the strings to dictate change, but you can create a supportive, transparent, and communicative environment for yourself and your team.

When you know a change is in the works, return to observing, listening, understanding, and connecting. Observe what's happening around you - maybe you're able to see something coming that hasn't even been communicated to you. Your third eye is hard at work through this phase. Listen for clues into what the future might look and feel like. What type of information, training, and support will you and your team need to manage through the implementation of this new shift? What kind of skills aren't up to par, and what would be helpful? Start lining up some support partners and mentors to get ahead of whatever this may be. Even if it doesn't move too quickly, there's never a bad reason to gain more skills for you or your team. Your understanding of the situation should start to develop, and asking the right questions will hopefully open up transparency surrounding anything that might still seem a little mysterious. And lastly, connect. You've done all that's within your control to move through this change as a leader. Provide a platform for communication to answer questions, offer guidance, and be honest when you don't know what's in store. Before any difficult conversations, doing a brief meditation to connect to your higher self for guidance and seeking the right words from the heart will be beneficial, and ensure you're working in an empathetic capacity.

• • •

You might have done all this work to be a conscious leader, and provide a great environment for your team, but what happens when you have a leader who has not? Don't forget to manage-up.

Managing up is the ongoing process of learning and working alongside your boss. You become acutely aware of their management style, brand of leadership, and build a rapport with them. You may not have a similar style, but you take care to work with them, understanding your own styles (and perhaps triggers). *To know thyself is to know others.*

You show up for them, exactly how you would want your team to show up for you. Ask what you can help with. Be honest in your communications. Be authentic in your interactions. Your leader needs to understand that you have discernment over what information is filtered down to your team. Show them this through shared communications and request 1:1s if you don't have them already.

As I work with leaders through a change initiative, the biggest concern is usually not making the decision to change, or even justifying the decision. It's "How will they feel?" Newsflash: You can't control how they'll feel when they become aware of the impact of change. But you can control the level of information, understanding, and clarity you extend behind making this big decision. The very question of 'how will they feel?' means that you're taking feelings into account. And that's about the most control you can have in the realm of others emotions.

You're better off starting with how you feel about the change. *Know thyself, and know others.*

Worst case scenario, the change is unbearable for some folks. With a communication plan in place, should your integrity ever be in question, those that aren't in alignment have something to fall back on in the steps and information that was considered when making this shift, and they know they'll have emotional support in any case.

Following the work of Kathie Dannemiller, a brilliant organizational development consultant, in order for change to be effective and widespread, dissatisfaction, a vision of what is possible, and action steps all need to be present, and more powerful than the resistance against that change to be possible and successful.

When you cultivate a team environment where there is room for discussion and open dialogue, you allow room for dissatisfaction. With your team's mission and vision as a compass to the work, you've already established a vision of what is possible. As you work through your lunar cycle manifestations, you're guaranteed to take the necessary steps necessary to move through a change curve. Resistance is the uncontrollable variable here. Resistance can be influenced by your ongoing support of your employees, your candor, and working with them 1:1 towards their own mission and vision statements (their personal and professional development).

Chapter 13
Being a Conscious Leader

What is a conscious leader? The definition will likely shift from person to person because our understanding and experience of consciousness is unique to ourselves. What is your idea of a conscious leader? Who in your life would you consider to be one, and how are you working to incorporate consciousness into your day to day leadership?

There are so many exciting things happening in the corporate space with culture, DEI, leadership, mindfulness, and intentional practice at work. And with that, sometimes these new terms can become 'trendy'. The way to ensure an ideology moves past a trend into regular practice and effective impact is to establish a structure, a plan, and a change management strategy, all in alignment with your mission and vision. This can happen at any level; within yourself, within your team, or within your organization.

The New Leader

I once had a client who was new to a leadership role. She was fantastic. Dedicated and conscious, but was moving from a colleague-relationship to a supervisor-relationship with her peers. She was scared AF. I coached her through an effective performance and disciplinary conversation for one of her direct reports that was very overdue, and had gone unaddressed by her predecessor for many years.

The biggest and most effective advice I gave her wasn't the format in which to provide the information, it wasn't the bullet points to stick to for the specific issues, it wasn't the avoidance of perceived discriminatory language; it was the advice to stick to the facts, and don't let the emotions of her employee to impact her message or intention.

We knew this employee would likely fly off the handle and that this would not be a well received conversation. However, my clients consciousness and ability to tie the issues at hand directly back to the impact of the person in concern, the impact to her peers, the impact to the business, and ultimate setting of expectations and clarity on direction moving forward (to my not so surprise) resulted in a reasonable conversation with an otherwise noted unreasonable person.

· · ·

When I followed up with her to see how this conversation went, she said "I just kept hearing your voice in my head telling me to keep it real, keep it purposeful." To date - maybe my most favorite feedback I've ever received.

Gossip Queen

The word "gossip" gets a bad rap. If you're curious by nature, gossip is *chef's kiss* so good. If it become a question of moral ground for you, and you find yourself involved in gossip, there's two things to consider:

1. Are you on the giving or receiving end?
2. What's the tea?

You see, gossip doesn't have to be a bad thing. In the corporate world, sometimes it's the only way to find out what's really going on behind closed doors (or behind Teams group chats). Considering which end of gossip you're on; Are you receiving it? Awesome. Now's your time to begin your 'investigation'. Perfect time to start observing, listening, understanding, and connecting.

What's the tea? How beneficial is the gossip you've found yourself in? Is it boiling hot and will burn your tongue? Better cool that shit off before really drinking it in. Before I found my corporate consciousness, I was hell bent on maintaining some sort of image that I interpreted was needed to be successful. This can, unsurprisingly, lead to a giant lack of boundaries; taking on too much, listening to others opinions without developing your own. What I noticed as I started bringing my spirituality and intention into my work day, was that my love for gossip didn't go away. It didn't need to. I used my powers for good! I started gossiping about all the partners I had that made my life easier. I would pass on information to trusted parties who I know would be immediately impacted. If one of my mentees was getting ready to hop on a discovery call with a new partner, we'd gossip about all of the ways that department aligned with their own mission and vision.

When you start living from this place of intention and authenticity, there's less consideration needed in what you feel is "okay" to say. I knew what I was saying and doing was in alignment with my ultimate mission and vision - and wherever that led me, was to the right place. Even if I didn't really know where that was leading. Ultimately, I knew that the person on the receiving end was getting some helpful and positive tea.

Start giving some positiviTEA (see what I did there...) and that's the only gossip you'll receive and continue to give.

Curiosity Killed the Cat, but He Had 8 More Lives Anyways

In my years as a corporate HR nerd, I operated under my own understanding of what 'reasonable' felt like. It was difficult to quantify, because I was largely working intuitively and by reading others' energies to respond in what felt like 'reasonable' way, given the circumstances. I had pretty good feedback throughout my career that I was understanding, fair, honest, candid, and a 'cool' HR lady (woop woop!). I didn't think I was doing anything too earth shattering - I was just being a person who understood the business parameters I was working under, and understood the people I was working directly with. As my career progressed, I went from having a separate 'work' and 'home' persona, into someone who was just one whole human being who happened to sit in a leadership chair. I created my own values, and stuck to them. It was in this wholeness that I found true success. Along this journey, I partnered with others who not only expressed, but lived those same values I'd established for myself.

Once I witnessed my own growth through confidence in my values and aligned actions, and had cultivated a strong support network, I embarked on a mission to help other professionals live and work holistically - to be their full selves at home AND at work.

. . .

My definition of a conscious leader is a person responsible for others' wellbeing who continually finds themselves and facilitates that in others. They understand the need to integrate emotion, experience, and intention into all areas of life, even the '9-5'.

Exploring the tools for growth and understanding comes along with an exploration of your inner intuitive gifts. One supports the other. Heal first.

On the pathway to healing, you'll start to understand where it is you'd like to make changes and truly grow in your life. Alignment falls into place as the healing continues. Where the true magic happens is in cultivating that intentional life you've developed. This becomes so much more than a self-help journey, because you've brought in all different levels of support to help you get to that next-level place. These support relationships are not one way. Your energy is shared between one another. Healing yourself means healing your community. *To know thyself, is to know others.* You have to be a little selfish, to eventually save the world!

Finding your true self requires a playful (or sometimes desperate) curiosity. I've met plenty of leaders who step into a role with little desire to understand who they truly are, much less bring that to work with them. That's fine - it's their thing. They're just not rocking nearly as hard as they could otherwise in the leadership game, and I certainly don't think they're the ones picking up this book (and you think they're even having as much fun as you?!)

Sometimes that curiosity is a natural part of who you are - always seeking that missing piece. Other times life-changing events force us to reconsider our current standing in life and career, and we develop the need to do an evaluation of ourselves. Regardless of what brought you to this point of spiritual and intentional self-discovery, thank you for choosing the path of wholeness, not only for yourself, but for those around you at work and at home. Now, go be magical!

Transformed Lives

"My entire life I always felt and experienced things that most couldn't explain. I always questioned what I was experiencing, which affected my confidence to interpret what was actually happening, and I still didn't know how to navigate my gifts. Lindsay helped me get to a place that I had never been able to reach in my mediumship and spiritual journey. She has helped clear my energy in order to meditate. While meditating she has guided me through a spiritual journey that I didn't realize I could reach. This has helped my confidence in understanding my gifts and how to interpret my experiences."

Harnessing the transformative force of intuition, Lindsay partners with all those dedicated to their spiritual and intuitive growth, all the while fueling their enthusiasm for strengthening teams and communities.

"Lindsay was so warm and kind even though we had never spoken before. I have been seeing mediums since I was a teenager as it is common practice in my family and she made me feel more comfortable and confident in her skills than many. She was through and patient and I felt like I was talking to a long time friend."

www.lindsaymastro.com

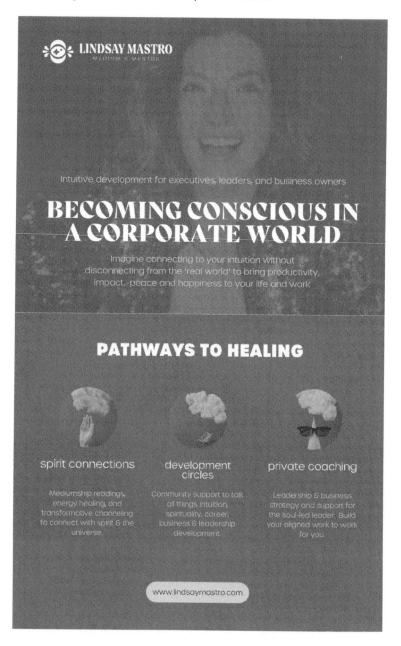

Made in the USA
Middletown, DE
15 September 2023

38573936R00130